111 LIFE LESSONS

GOLDEN NUGGETS TO ENRICH YOUR LIFE

BRAMARA SHIVANNA

I

Dedicate this book

To

Everyone

Who are interested in their Self Development

Contents

Contents

Contents

Contents

Contents

Contents

Preface

This book is compiled with the valuable information shared and written by many unknown authors. The stories are life-changing. We intend to bring these valuable golden nuggets to everyone looking for self-development.

Stories related to different areas of life like health, relationships, money, self image, acceptance, love, productivity, serenity, self talk, success and prosperity, many zen stories which are life changing are included in the book.

Acknowledgements

My deep-felt gratitude to my parents, siblings, husband, and my lovely daughters for the comfort and support they provided.

My gratitude to all my teachers, trainers, mentors, and Gurus who always came in timely manner to show the best path and provided me clarity on profession, passion, reality of life and shaped me up.

My gratitude to Meenakshi madam and all the individuals who has shared these stories in various whatsapp groups. Last but not the least, my gratitude to the invisible power of almighty and the universe.

Prologue

"You can't go back and change the beginning, but you can start where you are and change the ending."
—C. S. Lewis

CHAPTER ONE

EMBRACE YOUR IMPERFECTIONS

As we wade through life's muddled waters, especially as young adults, we tend deep down to be hopeful that we will eventually manage to settle down well and find perfection in a number of areas.

We dream of one-day securing healthy relationships, deeply fulfilling work, happy family life and the respect of others.

But life has a habit of springing surprises and rushing us in its overwhelming tide. It sometimes deals us a range of blows, leaving our dreams shattered. And like a favourite cup or plate, we sometimes crack. We may even break.

Obviously, you must not throw yourself away when this happens.

Instead, you can relish the blemishes and learn to turn these scars into art – like 'kintsugi,' an ancient Japanese practice that beautifies broken pottery.

In Zen aesthetics, the broken pieces of a ceramic pot should be carefully picked up, reassembled and then glued together with lacquer inflected with gold powder. The Japanese believe the golden cracks make the pieces even more valuable. It embraces the breakage as part of the object's history, instead of something unacceptable to be hidden or thrown away.

It is beautiful to think of Kintsugi as a metaphor for your life, to see the broken, difficult or painful parts of you as radiating light, gold and beauty. It teaches that your broken places make you stronger and better than ever before.

The times when you get hurt and broken, you can feel totally rotten. But there can also be a strange beauty in the way you process the cracks in your life and the lessons. you take from them afterwards. You can decide to cover up, or you can decide to walk out into the world as yourself, with your cracks shining in gold.

Embrace your imperfections and stay blessed forever.

CHAPTER TWO

MAGNANIMITY

Another trait, which is very important to succeed is to be Magnanimous.

For me, magnanimity is to be generous in forgiving an insult or injury; free from petty resentfulness or vindictiveness: to be magnanimous toward one's enemies.

Wikipedia defines it as 'the virtue of being great of mind and heart. It encompasses, usually, a refusal to be petty, a willingness to face danger, and actions for noble purposes.'

You may ask, 'What does magnanimity look like applied to daily life?'

Well, magnanimity is resisting the urge to take offense from other people's words or actions or not having to launch an emotional reaction to every perceived action or inaction or letting people go more easily than they thought you could.

The greatest temptation of life is to react immediately to stimuli.

This is Nietzsche's definition of the slave mentality: to be reactive, constantly responding to what other people say and do.

Magnanimity asks us to do otherwise. It asks us not to engage others on the immediate linguistic or emotional terms. And then, rather than jockeying for position, magnanimity asks one more thing, that we be generous.

To be magnanimous is to honour the other's state of being.

We've all had this experience of a parent, child, sibling, friend, spouse screaming at us out of frustration, anxiety, even well- deserved anger. We can, and often do reply in kind. They yell; we yell.

But magnanimity replies otherwise: it lets it all happen, lets the other person be, lets the other person express, feel, live while we only bear witness.

Son, You need to be Magnanimous in life, in order to move ahead and not let the actions of others shackle you in your pursuits and to maintain your peace of mind."

(An Excerpt from my Book, 'Dear Son....Life Lessons from a Father)

Searching for evidence of magnanimity in more recent times, I came across one name again and again: Abraham Lincoln.

During his lifetime and after his assassination, Lincoln was lauded for his magnanimity.

Some of the most poignant plaudits came from Lincoln's own would-be enemies. William Seward, originally a political rival and later Lincoln's secretary of State, called Lincoln's magnanimity "almost superhuman."

The president's relationship with another rival, Edwin Stanton, also stands out. An attorney general for the administration before Lincoln's, Stanton had earlier hurt Lincoln's law career by barring him from taking part in an important trial. Stanton even had a well-known habit of insulting Lincoln, calling him a "damned long-armed Ape," and "the original gorilla."

Nevertheless, Lincoln picked Stanton as his Secretary of War because he believed Stanton was the best person for the job. It was, according to one Lincoln biographer, "one of the most magnanimous acts of a remarkably magnanimous president."

We might expect that war, and in particular civil war, would stretch magnanimity to its breaking point. But the opposite seems to have been true for Lincoln. He could not put his ego before the needs of a riven country. The stakes were simply too high. "I shall do nothing in malice. What I deal with is too vast for malicious dealing," he wrote in 1862.

We may say that desperate times call for desperate measures, but for Lincoln they called forth magnanimity.

Be generous, Be Magnanimous and Stay Blessed forever.

CHAPTER THREE

ALWAYS PRAY WHEN IT IS CALM

There is a story about a sea captain who in his retirement skippered a boat taking day-trippers to Islands.

On one trip, the boat was full of young people. They laughed at the old captain when they saw him say a prayer before sailing out because the day was fine and the sea was calm.

However, they weren't long at sea when a storm suddenly blew up and the boat began to roll & pitch violently. The terrified passengers came to the captain and asked him to join them in prayer.

But he replied, "I say my prayers when it's calm. When it's rough I attend to my ship."

Here is a lesson for us..

If we cannot seek God in quiet moments of our lives; we are not likely to find him when trouble strikes. We are more likely to panic.

But if we have learnt to seek him and trust him in quiet moments, then most certainly we will find him when the going gets rough!

CHAPTER FOUR

WHAT DEFINES YOU?

What makes you shine from within is your virtues, your qualities, your strengths, the way you behave with others, and the way you treat them. Only the right ones can see that shine coming from you, and they help you shine even better because they also are good-hearted just like you.

You don't need the attention of the ones who do not understand your behaviour and see your qualities and strengths. If they fail to see your shine, the loss is theirs. You keep on shining.

The universe accommodates you for fitting in, but only rewards you for standing out.

Here's to all those who didn't believe in following the stereotypes and carved their own path. Only then they have created history and achieved success.

Never define yourself to comfort others' views about you. Have the courage to stand out, be companionate, love unconditionally, don't be judgemental.

Uplift others, it will never bring you down, it will instead make you grow spiritually and give you a sense of happiness and contentment.

The journey is not going to be easy however trust me it's worth it.

CHAPTER FIVE

THE FIVE-DOLLAR CHALLENGE

Most Stanford students fail this challenge. Here's what we can learn from their mistakes.

You're a student in a Stanford class on entrepreneurship.

Your professor walks into the room, breaks the class into different teams, and gives each team five dollars in funding. Your goal is to make as much money as possible within two hours and then give a three-minute presentation to the class about what you achieved.

If you were a student in the class, what would you do?

Typical answers range from using the five dollars to buy start-up materials for a makeshift car wash or lemonade stand, to buying a lottery ticket or putting the five dollars on red at the roulette table.

But the teams that follow these typical paths tend to bring up the rear in the class.

The teams that make the most money don't use the five dollars at all. They realize the five dollars is a distracting, and essentially worthless, resource.

So they ignore it. Instead, they go back to the first principles and start from scratch. They reframe the problem more broadly as "What can we do to make money if we start with absolutely nothing?" One particularly successful team ended up making reservations at popular local restaurants and then selling the reservation times to those who wanted to skip the wait. These students generated an impressive few hundred dollars in just two hours.

But the team that made the most money approached the problem differently. They realized that both the $5 funding and the 2-hour period weren't the most valuable assets at their disposal. Rather, the most valuable resource was the three-minute presentation time they had in front of a captivated Stanford class. They sold their three-minute slot to a company interested in recruiting Stanford students and walked away with $650.

The five-dollar challenge illustrates the difference between tactics and strategy. Although the terms are often used interchangeably, they refer to different concepts. A strategy is a plan for achieving an objective. Tactics, in contrast, are the actions you undertake to implement the strategy.

The Stanford students who bombed the $5 challenge fixated on a tactic—how to use the five dollars—and lost sight of the strategy. If we focus too closely on the tactic, we become dependent on it. *"Tactics without a strategy," as Sun Tzu wrote in the Art of War, "are the noise before defeat."*

Just because a $5 bill is sitting in front of you doesn't mean it's the right tool for the job. Tools, as Neil Gaiman reminds us, "can be the subtlest of traps." When we're blinded by tools, we stop seeing other possibilities in the peripheries. It's only when you zoom out and determine the broader strategy that you can walk away from a flawed tactic.

What is the $5 tactic in your own life? How can you ignore it and find the 2-hour window? Or even better, how do you find the most valuable three minutes in your arsenal?

Once you move from the "what" to the "why"—once you frame the problem broadly in terms of what you're trying to do instead of your favoured solution—you'll discover other possibilities lurking in plain sight.

CHAPTER SIX

THE SPIRAL OF GRIEF

Grief is not something we "get over" by following pre-prescribed stages, but a partner that we dance, play, honour, argue and weep with as the cycles unfold. Its appearance and the ways it longs to be tended are unique for each person.

The timeline for this voyage is not knowable by the psychiatric community, nor by insurance panels or teachers of spirituality, but is birthed and unfolds within the open pathways of the holy human nervous system. To rush, force, or pathologize the experience of grief is to work against nature.

The grieving process may not have an endpoint or state of completion in which we come to some final resolution, where we "finish" and land in some untouchable place, free from our embodied vulnerability, somatic aliveness, and from falling apart and breaking open yet again. For it is this alchemical rotation of vast cycles of rupture and repair that touch and open the human soul.

While it may be tempting to hold some fantasied end state as a goal which we reach as we "master" life or learn endless new metaphysical theories, the heart is not interested in mastery. But in entering, playing, and unfolding the mystery in more subtle and sensitive ways.

The heart itself is endless, and the visitors of grief may companion us in their various forms for a lifetime. They arrive not to harm but to reveal a portal into wholeness, mercy, and luminosity. Shifting shapes, circulating, and rotating, as they open and close passageways in the landscape of the interior pathways.

Grief is not so much a process that we "make it through," but a non-linear, purifying midwife and shepherd of the unknown. It moves not by way of the straight line, but by that of circle and spiral.

CHAPTER SEVEN

FALL BUT DON'T FAIL

"" Forget regret, or life is yours to miss, No other road, No other way, No day but today"
~Jonathan Larson "

It's important to remember that everyone makes mistakes and that everyone who makes mistakes has regrets. When you make a mistake, don't regret it and call yourself 'stupid'.

You are not stupid. You are just human!

Failures are the stepping stones to success. Without failure, we'll never learn how to succeed, try to fail, instead of trying to avoid failure through fear.

'Son, I have learned a lot of life lessons just seeing you guys grow up. Like when you were a toddler and trying to take your first steps and how you repeatedly fell down, yet got up and tried again and again and again.

Sometimes you laughed, sometimes you cried and at other times, you did both at the same time. But you kept trying and trying, laughing and crying. This was repeated several times in your acts while growing up, learning to speak, write, read, ride a bicycle and while playing tennis with friends.

Son, We did not label your experience as a "failure". We all just enjoyed your childhood.' Unlike us adults, babies don't know the possibility of failure, so they happily keep falling down until one day they take a few steps, and then a few more. Before long, they're jumping and running. All their trying pays off. They fall but never fail.

As grown-ups, what if we also simply choose not to fail? I always remember something my mentor used to say, **"The man who makes no mistakes does not usually make anything."** The only real mistake is the one from which we learn nothing. Treat your mistakes as a part of the learning process.

Life is a little easier if you expect a certain percentage of it to go wrong no matter how hard you try. A smart man makes a mistake, learns from it, and never makes that mistake again. But a wise man finds a smart man and learns from him how to avoid the mistake altogether. Fall but never fail, learn from your mistakes and stay blessed forever.

CHAPTER EIGHT

FUTURE IS A REPLICA OF THE PAST

Usually, the future is a replica of the past. Superficial changes are possible, but real transformation is rare and depends upon whether you can become present enough to dissolve the past by accessing the power of the Now.

Most people live in the past out of guilt or grief in the past or because of the same in the present life. Both these emotions are very destructive and take away the joy of today. If it is that we were very happy in the past and wish to stay back there to relive those moments, there is nothing wrong with that unless it eats up our present.

Being in the moment we are in, finding the good at this moment, this time will bring our happiness back.

Most humans are never fully present in the now because unconsciously they believe that the next moment must be more important than this one. But then you miss your whole life, which is never "now".

Forgiveness" is a term that has been in use for two thousand years, but most people have a very limited view of what it means. You cannot truly forgive yourself or others as long as you derive your sense of self from the past. Only through accessing the power of the Now, which is your own power, can there be true forgiveness. This renders the past powerless, and you realize deeply that nothing you ever did or that was ever done to you could touch even in the slightest the radiant essence of who you are. The whole concept of forgiveness then becomes unnecessary.

CHAPTER NINE

WRITE A CHEQUE TO YOURSELF

In 1990, while he was still relatively unknown, comedian Jim Carrey wrote a check to himself for $10 million for "acting services rendered." The check was postdated for Thanks giving 1995. As Carrey explained, it wasn't about money. He knew that if he was making that much, he'd be working with the best people on the best material.

Carrey earned about $800,000 for his work in 'Ace Ventura and 'The Mask.' Then, in late 1994, he was paid $7 million for his role in 'Dumb and Dumber.' In 1995, he earned many more millions and is now getting $20 million per movie!

Jim Carrey's "post-dated cheque" exercise is a great example of the power of the subconscious mind to actualize a goal that is held with deep conviction and feeling.

Thinking about your goal and forming images in your mind will go a long way to creating the success you desire. However, when you also use a tangible representation of your goal (such as a cheque), your chances of success are even greater!

I am not sharing this story simply because it's an interesting story about Jim Carrey. This same technique can work for all of us!

Why not tear out one of your cheques today and postdate it three or five years from now with the amount that you want to earn for "services rendered"? Make sure to look at that check at least once a day and believe that you're moving toward that goal.

So, is there a position that you want to achieve? CEO, Owning a business or a Successful Start-Up owner, a relationship you want to get into, a house you want to buy or a car you want to drive or that cruise you always wanted to enjoy? Whatever it is, create a visual aid and your mind will get to work to bring that picture into your life.

CHAPTER TEN

WE DO NOT SEE THINGS AS THEY ARE

""We do not see things as they are, we see them as we are"
we are"
--Anais Nin"

This is such a beautiful quote by Anais Nin! This is one of the most brilliant pieces of wisdom that, when understood completely, can liberate us from so much of our suffering.

We see the world through a sort of filter made up of all of the ideas and beliefs we created in childhood. When we started to observe the world as children, we learned how to earn love, acceptance, safety, and how to avoid pain.

When we look at an inkblot or a piece of art, let's say, what we see, how we interpret the object, comes from deep within our subconscious minds. That's why people see different things and react in different ways to art.

When you look at an interpersonal situation that triggers an emotional reaction for you, you are seeing something in the situation that is reflecting for you an issue in your subconscious belief system. The reason the situation happened to you, the reason you are having a reaction to it, is because it is asking for awareness. By bringing awareness to the internal emotional wound, or false set of beliefs (about who you have to be to earn love or avoid pain) you are healing aspects of yourself and bringing more light and more access to love.

The relationships that are most difficult, most trying, most emotionally painful, are the ones that are your greatest teachers. This is not to say that we should tolerate any sort of abuse or disrespect. But rather, instead of blaming "them," the wiser thing to do is to go inside and investigate what inside of us is reacting to them. What patterns or dynamics (always from childhood) are they bringing to the surface for us to see.

DREAM BIG

This quote by **George Bernard Shaw** offers me inspiration on difficult days when my goals seem too far away:

> ""*The reasonable man adapts himself to the world; the unreasonable one persists in trying to adapt the world to himself. Therefore, all progress depends on the unreasonable man.*" "

The Difference between winning and not losing is most often not quitting. It took Walt Disney 16 years to get the rights to make "Mary Poppins", now considered one of the best films of that time.

He was turned down 302 times when trying to find financing for Disneyland before striking a deal with the television studios.

And in the most unbelievable story, he was fired from his first job ever, at a newspaper for not being creative and innovative enough! He went on to own that same company.

Walt was able to keep pushing because he believed in himself and in his dreams, giving him the resilience to work hard and make them come true.

Steve Jobs laid out the success mantra beautifully when he said, *"I'd rather have average talent with a fierce heart that inspires me to be unstoppable versus being brilliant* – but frightened to do anything with it.

Press on. Nothing in the world can take the place of persistence. I'm convinced that about half of what separates successful entrepreneurs from the non-successful ones is pure perseverance."

Dream Big, Believe in your dreams & stay blessed forever.

CHAPTER TWELVE

A SMALL THOUGHTFUL SOLUTION CAN SOLVE MAJOR PROBLEMS

This was the Treasury room of a Wealthy King. Gold as coins, bars, and jewellery, Silver, and Precious stones like rubies, diamonds, sapphire, and pearls was being stocked.

The trusted Ministers entered, escorted by the Security Guards. The Ministers took an account of the stock, noting it in their diary, and left the room As they left, the security guards bolted the doors, carefully locked them, and checked if they had properly locked the room. The security guards pulled the lock to check and confirm the security.

As they left, it surprised them at a conversation that ensued behind them, They patiently listened to the conversation between the door and the lock! The door thundered, "What is the use of such able-bodied security guards? I am the biggest security, guarding the treasures of millions. I guard the king's richness and prosperity!"

The lock laughed, and said, "What use of being so pretty and ornamental, yet be proud of yourself? What do you guard without me? You have no value without me!"

The Security guards were pondering about the statements, and one of them dropped the key, and picked it up immediately, as he hand it over to be kept safely. He then wondered, without the key, you cannot open the lock and without that, you cannot open the door.

MORAL:

A door is much smaller compared to a house, A lock is much smaller compared to the door, And a key is the smallest of all. But the Key can open entire the House. So, a small thoughtful solution can solve major problems.

CHAPTER THIRTEEN

PICTURE YOUR WAY TO SUCCESS!

"You must first clearly see a thing in your mind before you can do it.
~Alex Morrison"

In a television interview, singer Celine Dion was asked if she ever dreamed at the start of her career that someday she'd sell millions of records and be on tour, singing in front of tens of thousands of people each week. The singer replied that none of this surprised her, as she had pictured the whole thing since she was five years old!

She was not bragging and has worked unbelievably hard to earn every bit of her success.

She learned at an early age that she could tap into the power of holding a vivid, powerful image... to picture the star she wanted to become.

World-class athletes also incorporate the power of imagery to reinforce in their minds exactly how they want to perform.

Whether it's a figure skater completing a difficult jump, a tennis pro acing his opponent with a perfect serve, or a golfer driving the ball long and straight down the fairway, many top competitors mentally envision a successful outcome before actually achieving it in the "real" world.

Visualization, however, is not something reserved solely for singers, athletes or movie stars. In fact, it's something we've used since childhood to create the circumstances of our own life.

Visualization is often described as "movies of the mind," "inner pictures" or "images." We all store pictures in our minds about the type of relationships we deserve, the degree of success we'll attain at work, the extent of our leadership ability, the amount of money we'll earn and accumulate, and so on.

But, we don't need to limit ourselves to our earlier images but can create new images for ourselves. We can make new mental movies whenever we choose to do so. And when we develop and concentrate on new images that evoke powerful feelings and sensations, we'll act in ways that support those new pictures!

So, the first step is to create an image of your desired outcome.

We are limited only by your imagination.

As you know, most people are terrified about public speaking. In survey after survey, it is listed as the #1 fear that people have — ranked ahead of the fear of death!

So, when most people are asked to even consider making a speech, what kinds of pictures do they run through their minds? They see themselves standing nervously in front of the audience.

Perhaps they're having trouble remembering what they want to say. Run these images over and over on your mental screen and you can be sure that you won't have much success as a speaker!

Instead, form a picture in your mind in which you're confidently giving your presentation. The audience members are listening to your every word. You look sharp.

CHAPTER FOURTEEN

ACCOUNTABILITY BREEDS RESPONSIBILITY

There is only one person responsible for the quality of your life. That person is **YOU**.

Taking personal responsibility is crucial in order for us to be successful, mediocre people don't ever take personal responsibility for their life. We cannot change either the circumstances, the seasons, or the wind, but we can change ourselves. That is the only thing we have to charge over. At the end of the day, our success is dependent upon us, so take every opportunity, rise up and take control of life.

Everything we do is based on the choices that we make. It's not our parents, our past relationships, our job, the economy, the weather, an argument or our age that is to be blamed. We and only we are responsible for every decision and choice that we make.

The victim mindset dilutes the human potential. By not accepting personal responsibility for our circumstances, we greatly reduce our power to change them.

Accountability breeds responsibility. In Jacob Nordby's words, "Among the greatest tragedies is a person who believes that they aren't meant to win, by winning. I mean find their purpose, passion, and joy in life. They believe that other people have better DNA or happiness genes or something, but that they themselves are missing a critical chromosome. This is a lie and it is begging to be unbelieved. For the moment we know the truth about ourselves, we can take both responsibilities for our own lives and inspired action to create exactly the life which is our birthright. In other words, you were meant to win."

Taking personal responsibility ensures that In the long run, we will shape our lives, and we will shape ourselves. The process never ends until we die. And the choices we make are ultimately our own responsibility.

CHAPTER FIFTEEN

ANT AND THE LENS

The Ant & the Contact Lens: a true story

Brenda was almost halfway to the top of the tremendous granite cliff. She was standing on a ledge where she was taking a breather during this, her first rock climb. As she rested there, the safety rope snapped against her eye and knocked out her contact lens. 'Great', she thought. 'Here I am on a rock ledge, hundreds of feet from the bottom and hundreds of feet to the top of this cliff, and now my sight is blurry.'

She looked and looked, hoping that somehow it had landed on the ledge. But it just wasn't there.

She felt the panic rising in her, so she began praying. She prayed for calm, and she prayed that she may find her contact lens.

When she got to the top, a friend examined her eye and her clothing for the lens, but it was not to be found. Although she was calm now that she was at the top, she was saddened because she could not clearly see across the range of mountains.

She Prayed to God ......Oh God, You can see all these mountains. You know every stone and leaf, and You know exactly where my contact lens is. Please help me.'

A little later, Another set of Hikers reached the top. One of them shouted out, 'Hey, you guys! Anybody loses a contact lens?'

Well, that would be startling enough, but you know why the climber saw it? An ant was moving slowly across a twig on the face of the rock, carrying it!

The story doesn't end there. Brenda's father is a cartoonist. When she told him the incredible story of the ant, the prayer, and the contact lens, he drew a cartoon of an ant lugging that contact lens with the caption, 'God I don't know why You want me to carry this thing. I can't eat it, and it's awfully heavy. But if this is what You want me to do, I'll carry it for You.'

I think it would do all of us some good to say, " God , I don't know why You want me to carry this load. I can see no good in it and it's awfully heavy. But, if You want me to carry it, I will ".

God doesn't call the qualified, He QUALIFIES those He calls

LOOKING AT LIFE DIFFERENTLY

There was an aged artist who lived in a small village. The man used to design beautiful artworks to be sold at an attractive price.

One day, a poor man among the villagers challenged the old man saying: "You earn a lot of money from your handiwork but why don't you assist poor people in the village?

Can't you see that the butcher is not as rich as you are, but he still shares free meat with the poor people in the village? Also, look at the village baker. He is a poor man with a large family. Yet he gives the poor people free loaves of bread".

The artist did not respond angrily to the accusations. He only smiled.

The poor man was confused about the reaction of the artist so he left him and went out spreading rumours that the artist was so rich, but he was a selfish person who only accumulated wealth and refused to help the poor.

The villagers hated the old sirtist and they all forsook him.

The old artist became sick and could not do anything for himself but nobody among the villagers cared to visit him or helped him so he died a lonely old man.

The days passed by and the villagers observed that the butcher stopped the free distribution of meat and the baker could not give the poor people free loaves of bread anymore.

When the butcher and the baker were asked why they stopped helping the villagers, they said that: "the old artist used to donate money every month to pay for the free meat and bread to the poor people in the village. Now that he was dead, there was nobody to pay for the free food anymore"

Actually, many people may have wrong impressions and different opinions about you. But do not allow any of them to influence or destroy who you are.

Do not pass judgment on anyone based on his physical appearance or what people say about him.

There are things about his personal life you do not know. If you were privileged to know about them, your judgment would surely be different.

A man died in a drinking- spot/dance hall. Another person died in the Church. If we are to judge them, we would say that the 1st man died a sinner and the 2nd man died a righteous man.

But the 1st man entered the drinking spot to preach against sin and the 2nd man entered the Church to steal from church.

For this reason, you and I cannot decide who goes to heaven or who goes to hell.

Fear God in your privacy and fear God in the open.

Human physical appearance is just a deception therefore forgive people and ignore their shortcomings.

Pray for one another. Be good to everybody. And don't cut off your relationship with a person just because he does not please you.

Establish unity and harmony with all.

For the LORD Who created all souls, knows what each soul conceals.

CHAPTER SEVENTEEN

WHY ME?

One of the Best Messages which I Received and which Explains Life... Completely True and the Best...

Arthur Ashe, The Legendary Wimbledon Player was dying of AIDS which he got due to Infected Blood he received during Heart Surgery in 1983.

He received letters from his fans, one of which conveyed: "Why did God have to select you for such a bad disease??"

To this Arthur Ashe replied:

50 million children started playing Tennis

5 Million learnt to play Tennis, 5,00,000 learnt Professional Tennis, 50,000 came to Circuit,

5,000 reached Grandslam,

50 reached Wimbledon,

4 to the Semifinals,

2 to the Finals

When I was holding the Cup I never asked God " Why Me?" and now in Pain, I should not be asking God 'Why Me ?'

Happiness keeps U Sweet!!

Trials keep U Strong!!

Sorrows keep U Human!!

Failure keeps U Humble!!

Success keeps U Glowing but
only Faith keeps U Going.....
So have Hope in Heart and Faith in God , don't think "
Why Me?"

CHAPTER EIGHTEEN

RIGHT AND WRONG

When Bankei a Zen Teacher held his seclusion weeks of meditation, pupils from many parts of Japan came to attend. During one of these gatherings, a pupil was caught stealing. The matter was reported to Bankei with the request that the culprit is expelled. Bankei ignored the case.

Later the pupil was caught in a similar act, and again Bankei disregarded the matter. This angered the other pupils, who drew up a petition asking for the dismissal of the thief, stating that otherwise, they would leave the Master.

When Bankei had read the petition he called everyone before him. "You are wise brothers," he told them. "You know what is right and what is not right. You may go somewhere else to study if you wish, but this poor brother does not even know right from wrong. Who will teach him if I do not? I am going to keep him here even if all the rest of you leave."

A torrent of tears cleansed the face of the brother who had stolen. All desire to steal had vanished.

Explanation: This story is pretty straightforward, but it certainly doesn't make you think any less than the rest. How quickly would most people turn their back on those who commit a crime like stealing, just as the pupils did? But look deeper and you might just see another human being. Someone that simply needs to be shown the path.

Don't write people off so easily. Expressing compassion isn't always easy, but we're all together in this life, so we can't just help those that keep good behaviour. Those people who commit such crimes are often some of the people that need help with the most basic spiritual and human principles, such as right and wrong.

If you have a loved one who's committed a crime before you'll know exactly what I mean. You know they can be better and they shouldn't be thrown out just because they did something wrong at some point. Sure, we need to keep order, so they should be disciplined for their behavior, but we also need to take the time to teach them right and wrong. We should strive to lift them up just as we strive to lift ourselves and those we love up despite their own flaws.

CHAPTER NINETEEN

THE SEED OF SAINTHOOD

One night a thief entered the hut of the Saint, Pavhari Baba, while he was sleeping. The thief had picked up a few things and was putting them in a bundle when Pavhari Baba woke up. They dropped the bundle in fright and fled.

Pavhari Baba picked up the bundle and ran after the man. When he finally caught up with him he said, 'Lord, you were gracious enough to come to my house, but why did you go away leaving these things behind?"

In Pavhari Baba's eyes, the man was not a thief, but God, his own Chosen Ideal. He insisted that the man take the things he had tried to steal.

Seeing Pavhari Baba's loving behaviour, the thief felt repentant. From that day he gave up his criminal activities and eventually became a holy man.

When Swami Vivekananda was wandering in the Himalayas he came upon a group of holy men. Among them, he noticed one, with an exceptionally serene appearance who seemed to be a great Saint. After Swamiji had conversed with him for some time, he realized that this was the man who had tried to steal from Pavhari Baba. He was speechless with wonder.

As Swamiji continued to talk with him, he understood that the man was indeed a man of high Spiritual attainments. Because of this incident, Swamiji would often say that even in the worst sinner there is the seed of Sainthood.

CHAPTER TWENTY

GLAD AND SAD

A merchant had to travel a trade route across the desert. He travelled from village to village selling goods off the back of his camel.

On one trip, a sandstorm kicked up and covered the trail. He wandered around looking for the familiar route.

When he ran out of water, he began to worry. Eventually, he saw in the distance what looked like an oasis. He moved as fast as he could to what could be his salvation.

Just as darkness fell, he felt cool water on his sandal. He dropped to his knees and began cupping water into his mouth with his palm thanking God that he had survived.

Then, out of the darkness, he heard a big booming voice from heaven say, "Merchant! Reach down, pick up some stones, put them into your pocket, and in the morning you will be both glad and sad."

Well, when a big booming voice from heaven tells you to do something, you tend to do it. So, he reached into the stream, picked up a few pebbles, and put them into his pocket. He then packed up his camel as fast as he could and took off.

When he felt like he was far enough away from the voice that he was safe, he made camp. Laying under the stars, he finally realized that he had been pretty dehydrated. So, he convinced himself that he had just imagined the voice.

When he woke the next morning, he felt something in his trouser pocket. He pulled the pebbles out of his pocket in amazement. They weren't just ordinary pebbles.

They were precious gems — diamonds, emeralds, sapphires, rubies...

At that moment, he was both glad and sad. He was glad that he picked a few pebbles up. He was also very sad, though, that he hadn't picked up more while he was there.

MORAL

Don't you always lookback and wish that if you had worked a little harder you could have developed more?.

CHAPTER TWENTY-ONE

THE 40% RULE

Jesse Itzler, the co-founder of Marquis Jet, talks about mental toughness in his book, 'Living with a SEAL.' While running a 100-mile race as part of a six-person relay team, Itzler met David Goggins, a Navy SEAL who was running the entire race by himself.

Running the race solo was a massive feat on its own-- and then Itzler came to realize that Goggins was running despite a damaging set of circumstances. Not only did Goggins run the ultra-marathon with broken bones and while weighing over 200 pounds, but he did so while suffering from an endurance-limiting atrial septum defect caused by a hole in the wall of his heart.

After the race was over, Itzler hired Ironman triathlete David Goggins, the world record holder for most pull-ups done in 24 hours and finisher of the 135-mile race in Death Valley (Goggins finished in fifth place) to live with him and his family in an effort to learn more about mental toughness.

While Goggins was living with Itzler, he taught him the "40 percent rule: When your mind is telling you you're done, you're really only 40 percent done."

Itzler then explained how Goggins showed Itzler that he could actually do 100 pull-ups, despite nearly quitting after completing only eight.

The human body is capable of amazing physical deeds. Pain is not something you want to avoid all the time, because when we continuously subject ourselves to it, we only grow stronger. If we could just free ourselves from our perceived limitations and tap into our internal fire, the possibilities are endless.

Train your mind and your body will follow beyond imaginable limits to achieve the impossible.

You will do well to remember **'The 40% rule** which is a term used to explain that when your mind and body are starting to tire and you feel like giving up, you're only at 40 percent of what you are truly capable of achieving. The 40% rule reminds us that no matter how exhausted we might feel, it is always possible to draw on an untapped reserve of energy, motivation, and drive that we all possess.

The reason why this happens is that our brain instinctively sets up boundaries and barriers to protect us from uncomfortable and harmful situations, whether this is by making us physically exhausted or pushing limiting beliefs to the front of our head, whereas when your mind is telling us that we are done, we are only forty percent done.

Our mind has a huge advantage over us. It knows our fears, it knows our insecurities and all of the self-doubts that have the ability to stop us in our tracks and make us give up. The only way that we can combat this is to build the mental toughness and fortitude to take back control of our minds and ultimately, our life.

Look at it this way, most modern cars have a setting on them called a speed limiter, which is what the factories set to stop you from using your car at its highest speed, for your safety and the car's longevity. Hence, you never get to experience the true power of your car. As soon as you turn off this setting, your car might be under a little bit more stress but, you can unleash its full potential and achieve more with it, just like your brain.

Try overcoming the 40 % rule in your own life, whether it's during exercise, in relationships, or in business. Challenge yourself to dig deeper, and ignore the mental limits and you will place yourself on the road to success.

This weekend, To make a new you, get in charge of your brain and strive to overcome your 40% barrier and stay blessed forever.

CHAPTER TWENTY-TWO

ENCOURAGE SOMEONE IN LOVE TODAY

"Barely three weeks after my son's wedding and honeymoon, I noticed a rather unusual pattern of him "stopping by" my place on his way home in the evenings. I thought he was just missing his original home. I asked him why but he gave no reasonable answer. He always asked for dinner when he came around, which was rather odd for a newly married man.

On his fourth visit, he came with one of his friends who were well known to me. I confided in his friend, who simply told me that his new wife "cannot cook". In fact, on the days he doesn't stop by, he eats at that friend's house or he eats out.

This was a fire on the mountain, the choice was between me encouraging him to eat outside at another household and risk ending his marriage or saving the day. I opted for the latter.

When he showed up again on Friday evening, I told him to tell his wife to see me on Saturday morning, we needed to go somewhere together, it was a woman's thing. She came as I requested and I told her I was entertaining my Church Society members and needed to cook for them. She was to assist me with shopping for the cooking. I noticed the fright on her face.

After returning home from the shopping, I told her she wasn't cooking because the people involved had very peculiar tastes, she was however to pay attention to all that I did in the kitchen. We finished (or I finished) all the cooking in about four hours. I made four different soups that I knew my son loved, made different stews with chicken, fish and beef and steaming rolls of rice.

After finishing, I told her to divide everything we cooked into two equal portions. She was surprised when I told her to take one portion with her when she was going home. I knew the food would last about six weeks, and as predicted, my son did not show up at my door until week seven. I knew the food had finished. So I repeated the same process again, telling him to tell his wife to see me when he got home.

By the third time we did this, I let her do the cooking whilst I supervised her. I never mentioned anything to her. By the fifth time, she had gotten a hang of things, even better than I imagined. On her way home, she hugged me passionately and said "Thank you Mum, you saved my marriage and you never even scolded me."

I am told that with my son's encouragement, she is now contemplating on opening a restaurant.

Rather than being the catalyst to scatter my son's marriage, I opted for encouraging them in love for them to attain a better and deeper understanding."

Encourage someone in love today, you just might be saving something very fundamental.

CHAPTER TWENTY-THREE

HATE IS HEAVY, LET IT GO

In my opinion letting go is something much easier said than done. The meaning of letting go is to basically take the thing you are holding onto and keeping current in your head (usually something negative) putting it into a helium balloon and releasing it. That thought is gone you have no control over where it goes but it is no longer something that you can dwell on or overthink because it's gone. It takes a strong person to be able to "let it go".

If you want to forget something or someone, never hate it, or never hate him/her. Everything and everyone that you hate is engraved upon your heart; if you want to let go of something, if you want to forget, you cannot hate.

When you hold resentment or hatred toward another, you are bound to that person or condition by an emotional link that is stronger than steel. Forgiveness is the only way to dissolve that link and get free.

Hatred can be just one-sided and if we are the one holding on to it, we are the only one Who suffers.Hatred is a very negative, draining and damaging emotion. You can't possibly embrace that new relationship, that new companion, that new career, that new friendship, or that new life you want, while you're still holding on to the baggage of the last one. Let go... and allow yourself to embrace what is waiting for you right at your feet.

ACCEPTANCE

Once upon a time there was a boy who had a dog. The boy and the dog loved each other and played happily as dear friends. But one day the dog did something that the boy's parents didn't like. To appease his parents, the boy had to send the dog away. Years passed, and the boy forgot there had ever been a dog. But inside him, there was still a place where something was missing. When he was a man, the missing place called to him so strongly that he had to go in search of what it needed. His search brought him to the edge of a forest.

Not knowing why, he found himself just sitting, waiting. Slowly, gradually, two burning eyes appeared in the darkness of the forest. The young man waited. Slowly, gradually, a long pointed nose emerged. The young man waited. Finally, out of the forest, slinking, there came an animal: thin, scarred, muddy, matted with burrs. You would hardly know it had ever been a dog.

The young man greeted it softly: Hello, The ugly dog stopped, untrusting. The young man felt in his body the memory stirring of the good and happy times with his friend. He said to this animal before him: I want to know how it has been for you, all these years in exile. And in its own way the dog told him, this, and this. Sad, lonely, scared, bitter ... The young man told the dog that he had heard it. He heard all that it had gone through.

And with the hearing, the dog visibly softened, became warmer and more trusting. After some time, it came close enough to be touched. When the young man touched the dog, he could feel the missing place inside him begin to fill in. And soon after he took the dog home, and gave it a bath and a warm place by the fire - after it felt loved again - it was no longer ugly. It was beautiful.

When young, the boy had no choice but to send his dog away. He felt a deep void in him all the time but could not do anything about it. He had made a life for himself without the dog and unknowingly had learnt to live without his best friend.

But as they say, some places in our hearts are reserved for someone special and so it was with the boy. But he soon realized what was missing in his life. He had grown up, and had every material thing that he wanted but, he still felt the emptiness within him.

Only when he accepted that he still missed his childhood buddy, that he was propelled to do something about it. And when there is a will, there is a way. So he found his dog. Life came a full circle for him when he accepted how much he missed a part of himself.

When we break up with some friend or somebody who at some time used to be very close to us, they take away with them a part of our heart and nobody else can fill up that emptiness. At times our ego stops us from acknowledging that we still miss the person.

Even though we may have been right in the situation that led to a breakup, we become the bigger and better person by trying to patch up. Accept that we were wrong and that we miss them.Don't let somebody who you love and who loves you walk away.

CHAPTER TWENTY-FIVE

TRY THE ELIMINATION DIET

Remove anger, regret, resentment, guilt, blame, and worry. Then watch your health, and life, improve.

Illness rarely arises out of the blue. It is usually the culmination of a string of poor lifestyle choices; really, bad habits. When we think of bad habits though, we usually think in the terms of those that involve eating habits or various forms of substance abuse. However, the bad habits that have the most profound effects on our health are the daily, recurrent diets of anger, regret, resentment, guilt, blame, and worry. These are the root causes of all other bad choices.

There is a specific portion of our brain, which is responsible for these negative feelings/emotions and the fight-or-flight reaction to danger that causes them. Eliminating them from our life will have a massive positive effect on our future success and happiness.

Pent-up anger can lead to self-destructive behaviours or explode into overt hurt to others. To eliminate it, we must first explore why we feel threatened; in other words, what is at the core of our rage? Regret is another powerful emotion that can freeze us in depression and despair.

To understand that the past does not have to predict the future is to begin eliminating this feeling. Being assertive removes the resentment that develops when we do something that we really do not want to do so as to avoid the pain of sticking up for ourselves. It is very different from being aggressive. We need to learn the difference and begin the elimination process.

Similarly understanding that the guilt is not really our guilt, but based on an arbitrary/manipulative set of rules usually established by someone else, can help to eliminate it. Our brain will cause us to look for blame for things that are out of our control to protect our sense of self. We need to eliminate this whole gamut of the blame game.

And last but certainly not least is to eliminate worry. No matter how hard we try, we can never know precisely what the future will hold. In order to prepare for this unknown of the future, we usually conjure up worst-case scenarios which manifest in the form of worry. This ill-fated attempt actually makes us less prepared as the anxiety it causes disrupts our sense of balance.

When we target these six and make a concerted effort to get rid of them from our life, it will work better than any diet, vitamin, or medication to move us into a state of health of mind, body, and spirit.

CHAPTER TWENTY-SIX

SELF TALK

How do you speak to yourself? But before you answer that let's see different ways we use speech.

1. Polite, courteous and at times in love with strangers.

2. Loads of patience, love and understanding speech with small babies and children

3. Taken for granted speech with parents and spouse

4. Preaching speech with teenage children

5. Naughtiness filled to irritate but underlined with love with siblings

6. Fun, no inhibitions speech with friends

7. Respectful and polite speech with extended family and elders

8. Hatred speech towards people whom we don't like.

99% of the time Self-talk is a combination of the 4th and 8th ways of speech listed above. We are most of the time either critical about ourselves, telling how bad and wrong we are or else preaching how it's necessary to change us.

Reflect do you really deserve this speech? Absolutely not. Speak to yourself with a lot of love and patience. Pat yourself for the good and point out the wrong but the way you would tell a small child or stranger.

Changing self-talk is the first step toward self-love. Take baby steps. Start speaking one good thing to yourself. Tell yourself daily at least 5-10 times about that one quality of yours which makes you unique.

For me, it's the compartments like trains I have in my brain and mind. They help me to detach.

Reflect on your unique quality and speak to yourself about it.

Whenever I feel a little lost and low, I tell myself you are unique because you can compartmentalise. This gets a smile on my face and peps me up... This works wonders.. Do try it out..

CHAPTER TWENTY-SEVEN

SMILE

A smile starts on the lips, a grin spreads to the eyes, a chuckle comes from the belly; but a good laugh bursts forth from the soul, overflows, and bubbles all around.

Think of the people you know who have great smiles. These smiles are warm, cheerful, and magnetic. How do those smiles make you feel? Happy? Hopeful? Special? A good smile can be really contagious to those who see it. If we all smiled a little bit more, maybe there would be a little more happiness in the world. A smile is happiness that can be found right under your nose. It can be the most beautiful thing in life.

A smile is the most beautiful curve on anybody's body, which starts from the lips and radiates through the entire persona. A smile if genuine, reflects in the eyes, it results in a grin for the person witnessing your smile.

A smile, a grin, a chuckle will soon convert into peals of laughter... A real throaty laughter which comes from a joyous soul. Laughter ignites a fire within the pit of our belly and awakens our being.

Laughter is God's hand on the shoulder of a troubled world. Laughter is the corrective force which prevents us from becoming cranks. Laughter is the foundation of reconciliation.

Each of us has a spark of life inside us, and our highest endeavor ought to be to set off that spark in one another. The person who can bring the spirit of laughter into a room is indeed blessed.

CHAPTER TWENTY-EIGHT

WHAT YOU WILL PLANT NOW, YOU WILL HARVEST LATER

What you plant now will determine what you will reap tomorrow...

A successful businessman was growing old and knew it was time to choose a successor to take over the business. Instead of choosing one of his directors or his children, he decided to do something different. He called all the young executives in his company together. He said, "It is time for me to step down and choose the next CEO. I have decided to choose one of you."

All the young executives were shocked but the boss CONTINUED. "I am going to give each one of you a SEED today - one very special SEED, I want you to plant the seed water it, and come back here one year from today with what you have grown from the seed I have given you. I will then judge the plants that you bring, and the one I choose will be the next CEO."

One man named Paul was there that day and like the others, received a seed. He went home and excitedly, told his wife the story. She helped him get a pot of soil and compost and he planted the seed. Every day he would water it and watch to see if it had grown.

After about three weeks, some of the other executives began to talk about their seeds and the plants that were beginning to grow. Paul kept checking his seed, but still, nothing shows on while others were talking about their plants, but Paul didn't have a plant and he felt like a failure.

Six months went by but still nothing on Paul's pot. He just knew he had killed his seed. Everyone else had trees and tall plants, but Paul had nothing. Paul didn't say anything to his colleagues, however, he just kept watering and fertilizing the soil he so wanted the seed to grow.

A year finally went by and the young executive of the company brought their pants to the CEO for inspection. Paul told his wife that he wasn't going to take an empty pot. But she asked him to be honest about what happened, Paul felt sick to his stomach, it was going to be the most embarrassing moment of his life but knew his wife was right. He took his empty pot to the board room.

When Paul arrived, he was amazed at the variety of plants grown by the other executive, they were so beautiful in all shapes and sizes. Paul put his empty pot on the floor and many of his colleagues laughed, a few felt sorry for him.

When the CEO arrived, he surveyed the room and greeted his young executives. Paul just tried to hide at the back.

"What great plants, trees and flowers you have GROWN," said the CEO. "Today one of you will be appointed the next CEO." All of a sudden, the CEO spotted Paul at the back of the room with his empty pot. He ordered the financial director to bring him to the front.

Paul was terrified. He thought the CEO knows he's a failure. The CEO asked him what happened to his seed. He told him the story.

The CEO asked everyone to sit down except Paul. He looked at him and announced to the young executive.

"Behold your next Chief Executive Officer, his name is Paul."

Paul couldn't believe it as he couldn't even grow his seed. "How could he be the new CEO?" another said.

Then the CEO said "One year ago, I gave everyone in this room a seed and told you to take the seed, plant it, water it and bring it back to me today. But I gave you all boiled seeds. They were dead and it was impossible for them to grow. All of you except Paul have brought me trees and plants and flowers. When you found out that the seed would not grow, you substituted it with another seed. Paul was the only one with the courage and honesty to bring me a pot with my seed in it, therefore he is the one who will be the new CEO."

SO LET ME TELL YOU

* If you plant honesty you will reap trust.
* If you plant goodness you will reap friend.
* If you plant humility you will reap greatness.
* If you plant hard work you will reap success.
* If you plant forgiveness you will reap reconciliation.
* If you plant faith in God you will reap a harvest.

SO MY DEAR FRIENDS BE CAREFUL WHAT YOU PLANT NOW, IT WILL DETERMINE WHAT YOU WILL REAP TOMORROW AND REMEMBER THAT WHATEVER YOU GIVE TO LIFE, LIFE GIVES YOU BACK.

CHAPTER TWENTY-NINE

SERENITY COMES WHEN YOU TRADE EXPECTATIONS FOR ACCEPTANCE

Our ability to develop and maintain meaningful relationships with others is often a primary source of satisfaction in our lives. One of the greatest causes of discontent in our lives is often the result of carrying too many expectations in these relationships. When we claim that someone has let us down or disappointed us, often times what we really mean is that they are not living up to our expectations.

Our ability to develop and maintain meaningful relationships with others is often a primary source of satisfaction in our lives. One of the greatest causes of discontent in our lives is often the result of carrying too many expectations in these relationships. When we claim that someone has let us down or disappointed us, often times what we really mean is that they are not living up to our expectations.

We become justified in our conviction that our way is the right way and blaming and criticizing become acceptable reactions when others don't do things the way we think they should. However, loving and respecting another person means allowing them to be whoever they are. In reality it's not the person that's letting us down but our own expectations of who that person should be that's letting us down. Letting go of expectations doesn't mean being defeated. If you are feeling defeated, you are still in a position of seeing things as right or wrong, black or white.

Letting go of expectations means accepting people and situations as they are. From this place, we can begin to appreciate others for being who they are.

It is like trying to pet a crocodile. When we try to do this and the crocodile bites us, we can't exactly blame the crocodile. The crocodile was just being a crocodile! We are wrong in expecting that the crocodile would be different, perhaps soft and fuzzy like a little bunny, and that expectation results in our getting bit.

Letting go of expectations does not mean we have to accept relationships or situations when boundaries are being violated, or abuse is occurring. We all have a choice to make when we feel someone has let us down or wronged us. We can either let go of our expectations, and our subsequent need to be right, and accept this person as they are, or we can decide this expectation is non-negotiable for us and we can walk away.

People rarely act and behave exactly the way we want them to. It's helpful to hope for the best and expect less, and remember that our personal happiness is directly related to how we choose to think about and respond to these challenging situations.

CHAPTER THIRTY

ZEN STORY: PRACTICE

Thought: If we look at life as a circular path, a line without a beginning or end, then we can learn to shift or focus away from the "final destination" at the end of the road and towards the gently curving slope of the absolute present moment.

One day a small boy was playing near the river when he saw an old man with a long beard seated in the sand. The boy moved closer and watched as the old man drew a perfect circle into the sand.

"Hey, old man, how did you draw such a perfect circle?" asked the boy.

The old man looked at the boy and said, "I don't know, I just tried, and tried again...here, you try."

The old man handed the stick to the boy and walked away. The boy began drawing circles in the sand. At first, his circles came out too wide, or too long, or too crooked. But as time went by the circles began to look better and better.

He kept trying and then, one bright morning, he drew a perfect circle into the sand. Then he heard a small voice behind him.

"Hey old man, how did you draw such a perfect circle?"

Reflection: This elegantly structured Zen story centers on the circle as a shape and symbol of perfection. The literal circle in the sand represents the necessity of repeated effort (practice makes perfect), while the narrative circle of the story (beginning and ending with a small boy on the beach) represents the circular nature of life.

Sometimes in modern times, we view success or perfection as a destination at the end of an arrow-straight line; we see ourselves at the beginning of the road, or the bottom of a mountain, and we can picture our destination clearly, glittering far away and out of our reach. In this mindset, reaching our goals can be intimidating, causing us to lose the focus needed to practice whatever it is we want to become better at, such as art, meditation, yoga, or perhaps attitudes of kindness and love.

However, if we look at life as a circular path, a line without a beginning or end, then we can learn to shift or focus away from the "final destination" at the end of the road and towards the gently curving slope of the absolute present moment. This viewpoint makes the journey towards perfection a little less imposing!

CHAPTER THIRTY-ONE

SUCCESS & PROSPERITY

" "Prosperity isn't defined by money alone;it encompasses time, love, success, joy, comfort, beauty and wisdom" ----- Louise Hay "

I once asked my mentor, "What really is the sign of success & prosperity?".

"There are several" he replied - "a smile of a loved one, contentment, freedom, the willingness to share, selfless service, fearlessness and the trust and confidence that you will get what you need in life.

Success is achieving small victories daily & prosperity is celebrating them."

Most of us miss out on life's big prizes like the Nobel, Oscar, Olympic Gold, Grand slam etc, but we all are eligible for life's small prizes -a hug from our best friend, a pat on the back from mom & dad, a short nap on a friend's shoulder, a glorious sunset, a chat with your loved ones, holding hands, a smile on your child's face, a moonlit night on the terrace, a sky full of brightly lit stars. a slow walk on an empty road with whom we Love.

Today don't worry about missing life's big prizes, but enjoy the small "REAL" ones & Stay Blessed forever.

CHAPTER THIRTY-TWO

AN 87 YEAR OLD COLLEGE STUDENT NAMED ROSE

The first day of school our professor introduced himself and challenged us to get to know someone we didn't already know.

I stood up to look around when a gentle hand touched my shoulder. I turned around to find a wrinkled, little old lady beaming up at me with a smile that lit up her entire being.

She said, "Hi handsome. My name is Rose. I'm eighty-seven years old. Can I give you a hug?"

I laughed and enthusiastically responded, "Of course, you may!" and she gave me a giant squeeze.

"Why are you in college at such a young, innocent age?" I asked.

She jokingly replied, "I'm here to meet a rich husband, get married, and have a couple of kids..."

"No seriously," I asked. I was curious about what may have motivated her to be taking on this challenge at her age.

"I always dreamed of having a college education and now I'm getting one!" she told me.

After class, we walked to the student union building and shared a chocolate milkshake. We became instant friends. Every day for the next three months, we would leave class together and talk nonstop. I was always mesmerized listening to this "time machine" as she shared her wisdom and experience with me.

Over the course of the year, Rose became a campus icon and she easily made friends wherever she went. She loved to dress up and she revelled in the attention bestowed upon her by the other students. She was living it up.

At the end of the semester, we invited Rose to speak at our football banquet. I'll never forget what she taught us. She was introduced and stepped up to the podium.

As she began to deliver her prepared speech, she dropped her three-by-five cards on the floor. Frustrated and a little embarrassed she leaned into the microphone and simply said, "I'm sorry I'm so jittery. I gave up beer for Lent and this whiskey is killing me! I'll never get my speech back in order so let me just tell you what I know."

As we laughed she cleared her throat and began, "We do not stop playing because we are old; we grow old because we stop playing. There are only four secrets to staying young, being happy, and achieving success. You have to laugh and find humour every day.

You've got to have a dream. When you lose your dreams, you die. We have so many people walking around who are dead and don't even know it! There is a huge difference between growing older and growing up.

If you are nineteen years old and lie in bed for one full year and don't do one productive thing, you will turn twenty years old. If I am eighty-seven years old and stay in bed for a year and never do anything I will turn eighty-eight.

Anybody can grow older. That doesn't take any talent or ability. The idea is to grow up by always finding opportunities for change. Have no regrets.

The elderly usually don't have regrets for what we did, but rather for things we did not do. The only people who fear death are those with regrets." She concluded her speech by courageously singing "The Rose."

She challenged each of us to study the lyrics and live them out in our daily lives.

At the year's end Rose finished the college degree she had begun all those years ago. One week after graduation Rose died peacefully in her sleep.

Over two thousand college students attended her funeral in tribute to the wonderful woman who taught by example that it's never too late to be all you can possibly be.

These words have been passed along in loving memory of ROSE.

REMEMBER, GROWING OLDER IS MANDATORY. GROWING UP IS OPTIONAL. We make a Living by what we get, We make a Life by what we give.

CHAPTER THIRTY-THREE

ENJOY THE JOURNEY

Let us accept the apology we never got,
Let us love somebody who loves us not,
Let us gift a dear one some distance and space,
Let us allow life to take its turns at its pace.
Let us be patient with our own mistakes,
Let us trust the friend who we know is fake,
Let us have the strength to be vulnerable,
Let us still be powerful enough to be noble,
Let us today make some promises we wont break,
Let us stick to every word we say for God's sake,
Let us laugh at our own weaknesses for once,
Let us not allow our flaws bother our loved ones,
Let us stop chasing life 'coz there is no need of catching
up,
Let us live as if God is really watching us,
Let us thank those who have broken our hearts,
Let us simply let go and quietly play our part,
Let us share some silence, today let us go away,
Let us stay less connected to the world for a day,
Let us meet the stranger within and start a new
friendship,
Let us embrace ourselves today into an eternal
courtship...

Let us live life like life for one more day, Who knows when death may arrive and quietly take us away?

CHAPTER THIRTY-FOUR

THE LIGHT

Ratan (name changed) was on his way home from the centre of his Grade 10 board examinations. His final paper had gone off well too. The previous day, he had ordered a DVD to watch once home after the examination. In the morning, he had told his mother to time a pizza delivery so as to enable him to enjoy the movie and pizza in his room.

At 2 PM, the pizza arrived home. 'Cheese Burst, Madam', the delivery boy reiterated. The mother collected the pizza.

Ratan would be home any moment now! Ratan did arrive. But he looked downcast and morose.

Mother knew better than to comment right then, though admittedly, her heart had frozen.

'Problem with the paper or what?', wondered Mother but was sure it couldn't be very bad.

'Ratan, your pizza is here. Your DVD must be on its way', Mother called out as the youngster entered his room to wash up.

Presently, Ratan came out of his room, picked up the pizza box and went to the main door.

Mother had made herself scarce at this point.

' Any bread and cheese in the house?', asked Ratan as he came into the living room holding a DVD in his hand. '

Bread and cheese??? I told you your pizza is on the table!'

Ratan shook his head sadly and settled down opposite his mother.

Mother could feel a knot tightening in her stomach.

' I came in an auto', began Ratan.

'Nothing unusual about that! You always take autos. What happened?', Mother spluttered on her panic-filled query.

'Mother, I was in the auto. Alongside me, a young boy about my age was riding his 2-wheeler. He was the delivery boy for my DVD. It was very hot and his shirt had stuck to his back with sweat. I looked at him enter the complex and walk towards our building. In fact, he came up in the lift with me.'

Ratan had tears in his large eyes and with his voice choking, he explained,' Mother, here was I, finishing my examination, coming home to a pizza and DVD. And there was he, delivering the DVD in this hot sun. I felt very sad, Mother.'

Ratan wiped his eyes, got up and told his mother, 'Along with the rental for the DVD, I gave him my pizza. Told him, my exams have got over. Let's celebrate! The boy took it happily, Mother!'

Ratan smiled at last and headed for the kitchen to fix himself a cheese sandwich.

'I did something right in raising my son.'

Mother felt entitled to say this to herself. Our Offsprings.

CHAPTER THIRTY-FIVE

THE INSPIRING STORY OF DR. MALVIKA IYER

Life may throw different challenges to different people, but ultimately it depends on an individual to provide a shape to their life, and in many ways define it. Bomb blast survivor Malvika Iyer serves as a wonderful example of survivors against all odds. Owing to a mishap, Iyer lost both her hands and sustained severe injuries to her legs when she was 13. She could not walk for the first six months, and after 18 months of hospitalisation, she taught herself to walk again and use a pair of prosthetic hands. "This was halfway into what was supposed to be 10th grade, but I had missed so much school that the only option was to lose more time," she shared while speaking to Humans of Bombay, a Facebook page that champions inspiring life stories.

Iyer did not stop at that. Not only did she clear her examinations but set a goal again for herself and got a state rank. After overcoming self-doubts and reading up about people with disabilities, Iyer realised, "like me, most of the disabled hated being pitied, we were alive and this was a celebration," she said. "In 2012, on the anniversary of my accident, after years of insecurities, hiding my new body, and a million stares and questions from strangers later, I finally wrote down what had happened and published it on my Facebook," she said. As luck would have it, the post went viral and Iyer was soon sharing her inspiring story with people all across the world. She has completed her PhD and is the first woman to receive the World Emerging Leaders award in New York. Last year, she was invited to speak at the UN Headquarters and co-chair the World Economics Forum's India Economic Summit in New Delhi.

In Malvika's words... "I was an inquisitive child — at 13, I was rummaging through my garage when my life changed forever. There had been a fire at an ammunition depot nearby that left fragments everywhere, and a grenade landed up in my garage — it exploded when I held it. I was rushed to the hospital, where by some miracle I survived the night — the doctors then began to piece me together. I'd lost both my hands and sustained severe injuries to my legs including paralysis of the nerves. For the first 6 months, I couldn't walk and was confined to a wheelchair. At some point, iron rods were drilled into both my legs. After 18 months of hospitalisation and surgeries, I would have to learn to walk again and use a pair of prosthetic hands. This was halfway into what was supposed to be 10th grade, but I had missed so much school that the only option was to lose more time — but I decided to take it upon myself to not. I shifted my entire focus to studying non-stop and enrolled myself in classes that trained me in crash courses. I was so determined that with the help of a writer, I cleared my boards — my first big victory! I loved that I had set a goal and achieved it so I did it again — and this time I got a State rank — I was even more motivated than before! I went on to study Economics followed by a master's in Social Work — those early years of college were the most difficult. I was on my own for a while and felt like I was surrounded by perfect people with perfect lives, while I was broken. I kept myself covered to avoid talking about what happened. It was hard for me to see myself as worthy. I felt incomplete. It was at this point that my family stood by me like a rock — they believed in me each day and cheered my every victory — I had to hold it together for them. It was also during this time that I met the love of my life who looked at me like I was the most complete person...my handicap wasn't even a factor for him —why was it one for me? I began to remind myself that my being alive was a complete miracle–if I got through my accident, I could do anything. I researched the life of people with disabilities. I realised, like me, most of the disabled hated being pitied, we were alive and this was a celebration.

I decided to celebrate myself — In 2012, on the anniversary of my accident, after years of insecurities, hiding my new body, and a million stares and questions from strangers later, I finally wrote down what had happened and published it on my Facebook — that post went viral! Soon I was giving my first TEDx talk and before I knew it, I had given over 300 speeches around the world. In 2016 I was awarded the first Women in the World Emerging Leaders award in New York and that same year I completed my PhD. Last year I got invited to speak at the UN Headquarters and even to Co-Chair the World Economics Forum's India Economic Summit in New Delhi! So this is my journey full of ups and downs — there were days I didn't want to live because the pain was unbearable. Even today, when I visit India, I face discrimination if I'm not wearing my prosthetics, but I'm on a mission to change that.

I take everything with a pinch of salt and anything new I do now is an adventure — at the moment I'm learning how to cook using my elbows! I want to show the world, that you being exactly who you are is your greatest power, and the way you look or what you 'lack' doesn't change that.

Look at me — I'm a PhD with no hands! Just know that a bad phase or a disability is a chapter in your book...it's not the entire story and the only person who can write your happily ever after — is YOU."

Develop and cultivate a firm belief, that When you accept yourself, you're invincible. To gain this kind of confidence, we may have to face years of struggle with finding ourselves and practising self-love.

I feel it's important for young people, especially if they are our future change makers or policymakers, to have an inclusive attitude towards anyone who is different from them in any way. People with disabilities need to be portrayed right by the media – not as a liability, but as a source of inspiration, as individuals who can equally participate in politics, governance, and any field of their choosing. Attitude is a very important concept, and we need to ensure that, when we are in a position to mould a young mind, we give them a wide perspective with regards to people being different, accepting everyone, and being more inclusive.

If you see a person with a disability struggling, ask them if they need help. Don't force help by taking it for granted that they are disabled and in need of help. Stop using restrictive terms for persons with disability. It is an irony that people in a wheelchair are referred to as wheelchair-bound. The wheelchair doesn't bind them. It liberates them. Don't stare. It applies to every person, be it with a disability or not regardless. Being curious is alright, but asking a person you hardly know questions like "Were you always born like this?" is not okay.

What we can do instead is, Share success stories of persons with disabilities. Be it at home, our school, college, workplace or community level. Ask persons with disabilities about their interests in all areas, not just disability. Having their voice in every medium is important.

People with disabilities don't come out often, as they don't have enough opportunities. Can we work together to open platforms and avenues for them?

CHAPTER THIRTY-SIX

FIND HEALING 'IN' THE TRAUMA

You do not heal 'from' trauma. You simply come to know yourself as Life Itself. And you turn towards the wounded place. And you flush it with attention, which is love. And maybe the wound will always be with you. Maybe you will always walk with the hurt. But now, you hold it. It doesn't hold you. You are the container, not the contained. It doesn't control you any longer, the wound.

Because it is drenched in awareness now. Drenched in You. Loved You. Even celebrated by You. You do not heal 'from' trauma. You find healing 'in' the trauma. You find yourself at trauma's sacred core. The One who is always present. The One who can bear even the most intense feeling states. And survive. The Indestructible One. The Infinite One. The Powerful One. You.

CHAPTER THIRTY-SEVEN

UNFORGETTABLE

An old teacher was being interviewed by a young professional. The professional started interviewing the teacher as planned earlier.

Young professional - "Sir, in your last lecture, you told us about "Contact" and "Connection."

It's really confusing. Can you explain?"

The old teacher smiled and apparently deviating from the question asked the young professional:

"Are you from this city?"

Professional : "Yeah..."

Teacher : "Who is there at home?"

The professional felt that the teacher was trying to avoid answering his question since this was a very personal and unwarranted question. Yet the young professional said: "Mother had expired. Father is there. Three brothers and one sister. All married..."

The old teacher, with a smile on his face, asked again: "Do you talk to your father?"

The young professional looked visibly annoyed...

The old teacher : "When did you talk to him last?"

The young professional, supressing his annoyance said: "May be a month ago."

The old teacher : "Do your brothers and sisters meet often? When did you meet last as a family gathering?"

At this point, sweat appeared on the forehead of the young professional.

It seemed that the old teacher was interviewing the young professional.

With a sigh, the Journalist said: "We met last at a festival two years ago."

The old teacher : "How many days did you all stay together?"

The young professional (wiping the sweat on his brow) said: "Three days..."

Old teacher : "How much time did you spend with your Father, sitting right beside him?"

The young professional looking perplexed and embarassed and started scribbling something on a paper...

The old teacher : "Did you have breakfast, lunch or dinner together? Did you ask how he was? Did you ask how his days are passing after your mother's death?"

Drops of tears started to flow from the eyes of the young professional.

The old teacher held the hand of the young professional and said: "Don't be embarrassed, upset or sad. I am sorry if I have hurt you unknowingly... But this is basically the answer to your question about "Contact and Connection ." You have 'Contact' with your father but you don't have 'Connection' with him. You are not connected to him. Connection is between heart and heart...

Sitting together, sharing meals and caring for each other, touching, shaking hands, having eye contact, spending some time together... All your brothers and sisters have 'Contact' but no 'Connection' with each other..."

The young professional wiped his eyes and said : "Thanks Sir for teaching me a fine and unforgettable lesson."

This is the reality today.

Whether at home or in the society everybody has lots of contacts but there is no connection. Everybody is busy in his or her own world. ...

Let us not maintain just "Contacts" but let us remain "Connected." Caring, Sharing and Spending time with all our dear ones.

CHAPTER THIRTY-EIGHT

PUT THINGS IN PERSPECTIVE

Eddie Rickenbacker, drifted in a life raft for 21 days, hopelessly lost in the Pacific. After surviving the ordeal, Rickenbacker said, "If you have all the fresh water you want to drink and all the food you want to eat, you ought never complain about anything."

The dictionary defines perspective as "the capacity to view things in their true relation or relative importance."

Just think about the people in your life. I know many people who lose their cool because they got a flat tire or some red lights when they are rushing for a meeting? I also know about those who sever ties with close family members because of a dispute over a small misunderstanding like the arrangements at a wedding or someone did not greet them warmly enough.

It's clear these folks have lost sight of the "relative importance" of things!

So, what is it that you've been complaining about lately? Are they really "life and death" matters? The next time you're tempted to gripe about your problems, pick up a pen and piece of paper and start listing all the reasons you have to be grateful!

Let me assure you, it sure beats complaining!

I'm not suggesting that you just sit back and ignore all of the problems in your life. However, rather than complaining, it's far better to focus your attention and your energy on those steps you can take to solve, or at least lessen, your problem. For instance, let's say you're feeling a little tired lately. Instead of telling everyone how lousy you feel, make an effort to exercise more regularly or get to bed a little earlier.

Complaints work against you in three ways.

First, no one is really interested to hear negative news about your illness and your problems. It's said that 90 percent of the people don't care about your problems and the other 10 percent are glad you have them

Second, complaining reinforces your own pain and discomfort. So why keep replaying painful, negative memories?

Third, complaining, by itself, accomplishes nothing and diverts you from the constructive actions you could be taking to improve your situation.

Seriously, all of us can cut down on our complaining and show some gratitude instead. At any point of time, our blessings far outweigh our problems, but we tend to focus on our problems instead. As Regina Brett, the American author said, "If we all threw our problems in a pile and saw everyone else's, we'd grab ours back."

For almost Forty years now, in times of stress and strain, when something has me backed against the wall and I'm ready to do something really stupid with my anger – a kind face appears in my mind and asks:

"Problem or inconvenience?" Will it really matter five years from now?

I think of this as the Test of Reality. Do your reality test every time you face any issue. Life is lumpy and a lump in the oatmeal, a lump in the throat and a lump in the breast are not the same. Learn to differentiate between a problem and an inconvenience and make life easy for yourself, make things work brilliantly for yourself every day.

From now on, let's do ourselves and others a favour and make our conversations uplifting. The people who don't complain very much and those who speak positively are a joy to be around. Decide to join that group so people won't have to cross the street when they see you coming!

Put things in perspective, ask yourselves 'whether it's a problem or inconvenience' and stay blessed forever.

CHAPTER THIRTY-NINE

HAWK & THREE FRIENDS

One day, two hunters came and sat under that tree. They were tired and hungry. They had not been able to hunt any animal. They decided to catch some fish. But, they couldn't catch even a single fish.

It was getting dark and the hunters decided to spend the night under that tree. To keep themselves warm, they lit a fire. The fire soared high. The hawk babies on the tree could not bear the heat and the smoke coming out of the fire. They started crying. The Hunters heard their cries. One of them said, "There are birds on this tree. Let us catch them. We shall roast them on the fire and eat them." The other one agreed.

The hawks heard them and were really worried about the safety of their babies. The she-hawk suggested that they seek help from their friends. The hawk went to the osprey and told her his problem. The osprey said, "Go home and protect your babies. I shall tackle with the hunters."

The osprey dived into the river and then flew over the fire. The water from her wet feathers fell on the fire. She repeatedly dived into the river and flew over the fire. The water from her feathers put off the fire.

The hunters decided to light the fire again; however, as soon as they lit the fire, again the osprey put it off.

In the meantime, the hawk went to get help from the tortoise. When the tortoise heard about the hawk's problem, he said to him, "Do not worry dear friend, I will be there in no time and tackle the hunters in my own way. Go and protect your family."

The hawk flew to the tree and the tortoise reached the tree. He went quite close to where the hunters were sitting and trying to light the fire again. The hunters saw the tortoise and one of them said, "Look there is a huge tortoise. Let's forget about the hawks and catch this tortoise."

The other hunter agreed and said, "Let's tear our shirts and make a rope. We shall tie its one end to the tortoise and other to our waists. Then we will pull the tortoise with all our strength." The other hunter liked the idea. Soon, they make a rope out of their shirts. They tied one end of the rope to the tortoise's legs. Then, trying the other end to their waist, they could not pull the tortoise. The tortoise's strength was much greater than the two hunters were together.

The tortoise pulled the two men into the water. Once, inside the water, it was very easy for the tortoise to drag them. With great efforts, they cut the rope that was tied to their waist and swam back to the bank. They were now feeling very cold. They had lost their shirts. They thought of making a fire again.

Seeing them collecting leaves and twigs, the hawk was worried again. He flew to the forest and called his third friend, the tiger. He found the tiger at the edge of the forest. When the tiger heard the hawk's problem, he immediately rushed towards the riverbank.

The hunter had now lighted the fire and one of them was preparing to climb the tree to get the hawk babies. Just then, the tiger reached the tree. Seeing the tiger, the hunters ran from there and never came back again.

The hawk thanked all his three friends for their kind and timely help. He also realized that it is very important to have at least a few friends. The female-hawk was very wise in advising the hawk to make friends before marrying him.

CHAPTER FORTY

PARADISE

"Paradise is not a place. It is a state of consciousness.
--SRI CHINMOY"

It's really remarkable how often we say, or we hear people say that they need an escape from life. People are always talking about vacationing to a warm tropical place.... Or as we all like to call it. Paradise. Is it really paradise? Is Paradise some place?

What if we made it a point to make our lives themselves our idea of paradise. A place we didn't feel we needed to escape from, a place where we weren't dreading coming home to.

We often lose sight of how much influence and how much say we have in our every day life. It's time we take that ownership and realize that. We are more than capable of finding that place in our hearts that can make our mind a conscious state of paradise, and it can allow us to get the most out of our days, and enjoy our days.

Paradise is a state of consciousness that we are capable of creating. For me, it is a state where you are unapologetically committed to living your truth and doing good in the world. It is a state of mind, accompanied by a serene, stress-free, and, most importantly, drama-free environment. Paradise is something I feel like I must work for. Something I have to earn. Kindness, compassion, helping others, not hurting anyone, having a sense of gratitude, spreading love and good cheer are some of the ways we can consciously create Paradise in our lives.

CHAPTER FORTY-ONE

THE STORY OF THE PENCIL

"What really matters in a pencil is not its wooden exterior, but the graphite inside. So always pay attention to what is happening inside you
----- Paulo Coelho"

A boy was watching his grandmother write a letter. At one point, he asked:

"Are you writing a story about what we've done? Is it a story about me?"

His grandmother stopped writing her letter and said to her grandson:

"I am writing about you, actually. But more important than the words is the pencil I'm using. I hope you will like this pencil when you grow up."

Intrigued, the boy looked at the pencil. It didn't seem very special.

"But it's just any other pencil I've seen."

"That depends on how you look at things. It has five qualities, which, if you manage to hang on to them, will make you a person who is always at peace with the world.

First Quality: you are capable of great things, but you must never forget that there is a hand guiding your steps. We call that hand God, and he always guides us according to his will.

Second Quality: now and then, I have to stop writing and use a sharpener. That makes the pencil suffer a little, but afterwards, he's much sharper. So you, too must learn to bear certain pains and sorrows, because that will make you a better person

Third Quality: the pencil always allows us to use an eraser to rub out any mistakes. This means that correcting something we did is not necessarily a bad thing; it just helps to keep us on the road to justice."

Fourth Quality: what really matters in a pencil is not its wooden exterior, but the graphite inside. So always pay attention to what is happening inside you.

Finally, the pencil's **Fifth Quality**: it should always leave a mark. In just the same way, you should know that everything you do in life will leave a mark, so try to be cautious of that in your every action."

Moral... When the same teaching is applied to life it would mean....

One: You will be able to do many great things, but only if you allow yourself to be held in God's hand. And allow other human beings to access you for the many gifts you possess.

Two: You will experience a painful sharpening from time to time, by going through various problems in life, but you'll need it to become a stronger person.

Three: You will be able to correct any mistakes you might make.

Four: The most important part of you will always be what's on the inside.

Five: On every surface you walk through, you must leave your mark. No matter what the situation, you must continue to do your duties.

Allow this parable on the pencil to encourage you to know that you are a special person and only you can fulfill the purpose to which you were born to accomplish.

Never allow yourself to get discouraged and think that your life is insignificant and cannot make a change life is insignificant and cannot make a change.

CHAPTER FORTY-TWO

ASK

The Sage said to his disciple, "I'll ask you one question. If you can answer this question, I'll know that you are ready. It is not a question from the Holy Texts and Scriptures," he added.

"On your way back to your village," the Sage went on, "will you pass a place where there are shepherds?" The disciple said yes. Then the Sage asked, "As you walk by this place where there is a shepherd with his sheep, if five of his sheepdogs attacked you, what would you do?"

The disciple said I'd pick up a stone and throw it at them." And the Sage said, "You might hit one dog, but the other four would still get you."

The disciple said, "Well, I would take a stick and try to keep them off?" And the Sage said, "I say to you again that you might get one or even two, but the remainder of the dogs would certainly attack you. I can see that you are not yet ready to go out to teach others in your own village."

The disciple said, "O Master, at least tell me the answer. The Sage told him that if he called out for the shepherd, the shepherd would come from his tent, and call each of the dogs by its name, and the dogs would turn away from the attack.

Then the Sage said, "In this world, there are people who will attack you like those dogs, and if you try to fight them off, they will win because they will outnumber you. But if you call out their owner if you call the One who created them, then He will call them by their name, He will make his presence known, He

will put them to shame and He will protect you."

We call God when we are in trouble. But do we call Him when we are not in trouble? Why not call him all the time? Why wait for trouble to come? Why not stay in his protective circle always...

CHAPTER FORTY-THREE

HOW TO CHANGE YOURSELF

"" change yourself and you have done your part in changing the world"

--- Paramhansa Yogananda"

Man is like a puppet. The strings of his habits, emotions, passions, and senses make him dance to their bidding. They bind his soul. A person's greatest enemies are his bad habits. They will follow him from one incarnation to another until he overcomes them. In order to free oneself from fate, he or she must do away with bad habits.

Good company is one of the best medicines. Be with people who have positive minds and with those who have the consciousness of success. Then you will begin to change.

The very nature of habit is automatic compulsion to do what one has become accustomed to do. Habits go on repeating their same old pattern, often ignoring a desire's new command. When bad habits are challenged, their self-preserving instinct makes them behave as though they were sufficient unto themselves to crush opposing good habits and intentions.

At the right time, and in the right environment, all good and bad actions of the past come to fruition.

Mental slavery to a sense habit is the result of continued repetition of the specific act that gives birth to a particular habit. Only when one pleasure after another fails him does man finally begin to wonder if, after all, happiness is possible through the senses. This thought has a liberating effect: man tries to find joy in meditation, in silence, in wisdom, in service, in contentment, and in self-control.

CHAPTER FORTY-FOUR

WHAT DO YOU PRACTICE DAILY?

"Every day brings a CHOICE; to practice stress or to practice peace"
    ---Joan Borysenko

I am sure that we have all experienced the stressful moments on a typical weekday morning when we are trying to cook, get the kids ready, get everybody to have their breakfast, get all the chores done before leaving for work...and the children, the pets, partner all choose to be difficult..... We get totally hassled and harried and unknowingly, our stress gets to our family too...

What happens is that we are everywhere but in the present moment, barking orders like a general and obsessing about the day's menu of events. And in the ensuing chaos of events, nothing gets done and we get even more stressed out...

We have to realize that the kids and the pets do not randomly choose that particularly busy morning to bounce off the walls. Instead, they are mirrors of our own crazed state: As we go off center, so do they. So the best way to change their behaviour is to change ours. We can try a stress-busting breathing exercise to start with and after just a minute or two of breathing in that conscious way, we would feel our energy shift. That scattered feeling of anxiety gives way to a kind of clear, focused energy.

Breathing is a unique physiological process that happens automatically, yet you can easily shift it with your conscious will. If you're stressed out, your breath reflects your mental state, coming fast and shallow, choppy and irregular. You may even unwittingly hold it for long periods of time. Stress breathing in turn stresses your body, causing it to release hormones that make it harder to concentrate and more difficult to remember things.

Every day brings a clear choice: to practice stress or to practice peace. I think, If we make a conscious choice to make peace of mind our primary goal going forward, everything else in life will flow more smoothly and harmoniously. Finding inner peace doesn't require hours of daily practice.

Life is a precious gift to be savored, not a series of chores to complete while you complain about being "crazy busy." Remember—your to-do list is immortal. It will live on long after you're dead. What matters is you, right now. So learn simple, effective ways to center yourself and bring mind, body, and spirit together so that life becomes a joy and a pleasure, and your best self can shine.

CHAPTER FORTY-FIVE

BELIEVE IN YOUR DREAMS

Once upon a time, there was a large mountainside, where an eagle's nest rested.

The eagle's nest contained four large eagle eggs. One day an earthquake rocked the mountain, causing one of the eggs to roll down the mountain to a chicken farm located in the valley below.

The chickens knew that they must protect and care for the eagle's egg, so an old hen volunteered to nurture and raise the large egg.

One day, the egg hatched and a beautiful eagle was born.

Sadly, however, the eagle was raised to be a chicken.

The eagle also started believing he was nothing more than a chicken. The eagle loved his home and family, but his spirit cried out for more.

While playing a game on the farm one day, the eagle looked to the skies above and noticed a group of mighty eagles soaring in the skies.

"Oh," the eagle cried, "I wish I could soar like those birds."

The chickens roared with laughter, "You cannot soar with those birds. You are a chicken and chickens do not soar."

The eagle continued staring at his real family up above, dreaming that he could be with them.

Each time the eagle would let his dreams be known, he was told it couldn't be done.

That is what the eagle learned to believe. The eagle, after some time, stopped dreaming and continued to live his life like a chicken.

Finally, after a long life as a chicken, the eagle passed away.

The moral of the story is that you become what you believe you are.

Whenever Iam reminded of this story, Iam reminded of another one I read recently.

Elon Musk had lunch with Charlie Munger, the renowned investor in 2009. Munger allegedly told the whole table all the reasons whyTesla would fail.

It "made me quite sad," Musk tweeted recently, "But I told him I agreed with all those reasons, but it was still worth trying anyway."

Isn't it inspiring.

So, if you ever dream of becoming an eagle, follow your dreams, not the words of a chicken or for that matter anyone else, even if he is Charlie Munger.

Follow your dreams, believe in them, achieve & stay blessed forever.

CHAPTER FORTY-SIX

LETTING GO

" "Let come what comes, let go what goes; see what remains"

-- RAMANA MAHARSHI "

When somebody told me that he has failed in his exams, my question is, "Is it a law that you will pass every time?"

When someone told me that her boyfriend broke up with her, my question is, "Is it a rule that you will have successful relationships everywhere?"

When somebody asked me why am I in depression, my question is, "Is it compulsory to have confidence all the time?"

When someone cried to me about his huge business loss due to his wrong decision, my question is, "Is it possible that you take all the right decisions?"

The fact is our expectation that life has to be perfect/permanent is the biggest reason for our unhappiness.

One has to understand the law of impermanence of nature.

After each sunny day, there has to be a dark night, and after each birth, there have to be certain deaths, for the full moon to come again it has to pass through no moon. In this imperfection of nature, there is perfection.

CHAPTER FORTY-SEVEN

ZEN STORY: WALKING ON WATER

" "The miracle is not to walk on water. The miracle is to walk on the green earth, dwelling deeply in the present moment and feeling truly alive."
--- Thich Nhat Hanh "

Three monks sat by a lake, deep in meditation.

One stood up and said, "I've forgotten my mat." Stepping on the water before him, he walked across to the other side, where their small hut stood. When he returned, the second monk said, "I've just remembered that I haven't dried my washed clothes." He too strode calmly across the water to the other bank and returned in a few minutes the same way. The third monk watched them intently. Figuring this was a test of his own skills, he loudly declared, "So you think your abilities are superior to mine! Watch me!" And scurried to the edge of the river bank. No sooner did he put his foot in than he fell into waist-high water.

Unfazed, he waded out and tried again. And again and again, to no avail. After watching this performance in silence, one of his fellow monks asked the other, "Do you suppose we should tell him where the stepping stones are?"

Seeking to perform seemingly impossible acts that cause wonder and astonishment will never trump the miracle of creation. We are naturally surrounded by the "miracle" of life and nature, on a beautiful blue planet, in which we have yet to find an equal in the universe.

Being present in this all-encompassing moment, this breath of life, this astonishing beauty of existence, is the only miracle to be aware of.

CHAPTER FORTY-EIGHT

BE GRATEFUL

There was a bird who lived in the desert, very sick, with no feathers, nothing to eat and drink, no shelter to live and kept on cursing his life day and night.

One day an Angel was crossing from that desert, bird stopped the Angel and inquired " where are you going?" Angel replied, " I am going to meet God".

So the bird asked the angel ' please ask God when my suffering will come to an end?' Angel said " sure, I will and bid goodbye to the bird. Angel reached God's place and shared the message of the bird to Him.

Angel told Him how pathetic the condition of the bird is and inquired when the suffering of the bird will go to end. God replied ' for the next seven lifetimes the bird has to suffer like this, no happiness till then'.

Angel said when the bird will hear this he will get disheartened could You suggest any solution for this?

God replied to tell him to recite the mantra ' **Thank you God for everything**. Angel met the bird again and delivered the message of God to the bird.

After seven days the Angel was passing again from the same path and saw that bird was so happy, feathers grew up on his body, a small plant grew up in the desert area, a small pond of water was also there, and the bird was singing and dancing cheerfully. Angel was astonished at how it happened, God told for seven lifetimes there is no happiness for the bird next seven lifetimes, with this question in mind he went to visit God.

Angel asked his query then God replied yes it was true there was no happiness for the bird for seven lifetimes but because the bird was reciting the mantra' Thank you God for everything in every situation.

When the bird fell down on the hot sand it said thank you God for everything, when it could not fly it said thank you God for everything, so whatever the situation may be the bird kept on repeating Thank you God for everything and therefore the seven lifetimes karma got dissolved in seven days.

When I heard this story it landed me in a different energy zone, I felt a tremendous shift in my way of feeling, thinking, accepting and viewing life.

I adopted this mantra in my life whatever the situation I faced I started reciting this mantra ' THANK YOU GOD FOR EVERYTHING. It helped me to shift my view from what I did not have to what I have in my life.

For instance, if my head used is paining I thank God for the rest of my body is completely fine and healthy and my headache does not use to bother me.

In the same manner, I started using this mantra in my relationship, finance, love life, social life, business, friends, maids, colleagues and everything with which I can relate. I shared this story with my spouse and children too which brought a great shift in their behaviour.

This simple mantra really had a deep impact on my life, I started feeling how blessed I am, how happy I am, and how good life is.

The purpose of sharing this message is to make all of us aware of how powerful the power of gratitude is. It can reshape our life.

A simple word, a simple thought, which teaches us to be grateful for everything that we have in our life has the power to dissolve the karmic baggage which we are carrying from so many lifetimes. Let's recite this mantra continuously to experience the shift in our life.

I end this article with the beautiful lines:

Be grateful, and see the change in your attitude. Be humble, and you will never stumble.

CHAPTER FORTY-NINE

SELF APPRAISAL

A little boy went into a drug store, reached for a soda carton and pulled it over to the telephone. He climbed onto the carton so that he could reach the buttons on the phone and proceeded to punch in seven digits.

The store-owner observed and listened to the conversation:

Boy: "Lady, Can you give me the job of cutting your lawn?

Woman:(at the other end of the phone line): "I already have someone to cut my lawn."

Boy: "Lady, I will cut your lawn for half the price of the person who cuts your lawn now."

Woman: I'm very satisfied with the person who is presently cutting my lawn.

Boy (with more perseverance): "Lady, I'll even sweep your curb and your sidewalk, so on Sunday you will have the prettiest lawn in all of Palm beach, Florida."

Woman: "No, thank you."

With a smile on his face, the little boy replaced the receiver.

The store owner, who was listening to all this, walked over to the boy.

Store owner: "Son, I like your attitude; I like that positive spirit and would like to offer you a job."

Boy: "No thanks,

Store owner: But you were really pleading for one.

Boy: No Sir, I was just checking my performance at the job I already have. I am the one who is working for that lady, I was talking to!"

This is what we call 'Self Appraisal'

Carry out your self appraisal , identify your weaknesses, the areas you need to improve & stay blessed forever.

CHAPTER FIFTY

A MOMENT TO BREAK ...

This is a true story that happened in Japan.

In order to renovate the house, someone in Japan breaks open the wall. Japanese houses normally have a hollow space between the wooden walls. When tearing down the walls, he found that

there was a lizard stuck there because of a nail from outside hammered into one of its feet. He sees this, feels pity, and at the same time curious, as when he checked the nail, it was nailed 5 years ago when the house was first built !!!

What happened?

The lizard has survived in such a position for 5 years! In a dark wall partition for 5 years without moving,

it is impossible and mind-boggling. Then he wondered how this lizard survived for 5 years! without moving a single step, since its foot was nailed.

So he stopped his work and observed the lizard, what it has been doing, and what and how it has

been eating. Later, not knowing from where it came, appears another lizard, with food in its mouth.

Ah! He was stunned and touched deeply.

For the lizard that was stuck by a nail, another lizard has been feeding it for the past 5 years. Imagine? it has been doing that untiringly for 5 long years, without giving up hope on its partner. Imagine what a small creature can do that a creature blessed with a brilliant mind can't.

Please never abandon your loved ones

Lesson from the Story:

Never Say you are Busy When They Really Need You. You May Have The Entire World At Your Feet. But You Might Be The Only World To Them. A Moment of negligence might break the very heart which loves you thru all odds. Before you say something just remember.

" It takes a moment to Break but an entire lifetime to make"

CHAPTER FIFTY-ONE

DARE TO REACH OUT

*"Dare to reach out your hand into the darkness, to pull another
hand into the light.
NORMAN B. RICE"*

By healing the souls of the wounded, we in turn aid in our own healing process.

By helping a lost individual find their place in the world, we better understand our own.

By helping an insecure heart see and accept its worth as a human being, we reaffirm our own value.

Through the simplest of acts, one can pull a troubled soul of it's hole.

By aiding others, we cause the seemingly evading darkness which surrounds us to dissipate.

Never underestimate the positive effect you have on others.

Your ability to perform well in this world is omnipotent.

""Thousands of candles can be lit from a single candle, and the life of the candle will not be shortened. happiness never decreases by being

shared." – Buddha"

So share your light; feed the dying flame of another.

Let your very essence flow into those around you; give unconditionally – because you can. Because it can do no harm. Because you can do so much right by touching the life of another. The lights will never go out, so long as we continue to share them.

CHAPTER FIFTY-TWO

VALUE YOUR LIFE PARTNER

One day, during an evening class for adults, the psychology Teacher entered the class and told students, "Let's all play a game!" " What Game?"

The Teacher asked one of the students to volunteer. A lady, Aliza came forward. The Teacher asked her to write 30 names of the most important people in her life on the blackboard.

Aliza wrote the names of her family members, relatives, friends, colleagues and neighbours.

The Teacher told her to erase 3 names that Aliza considered most unimportant.

Aliza erased the names of her colleagues.

The Teacher again told her to delete 5 more names. Aliza erased her neighbours' names.

This went on until there were just four names left on the blackboard.

These were the names of her mother, father, husband and only son...

The entire class became silent realizing that this wasn't a game anymore for Aliza alone.

Now, The Teacher told her to delete two more names.

It was a very difficult choice for Aliza.

She unwillingly deleted her parents' names.

"Please delete one more," said the Teacher.

Aliza became very nervous and with trembling hands and tears in her eyes, she deleted her son's name. Aliza cried painfully...

The Teacher told Aliza to take her seat. After a while Teacher asked "why your husband??

The parents are the ones that nurtured you, and the son is the one you gave birth to.

And you can always find another husband !!!"

Total silence in the class.

Everyone was curious to know her response. Aliza calmly and slowly said, "One day my parents will pass away before me. My son may also leave me when he grows old, for his studies or business or whatever reason. The only one who will truly share his entire life with me is and will be my Husband".

All the students stood up and applauded her for sharing this truth of life.

This is true. So always value your life partner, it's not only for husbands, it applies to wives as well.

God has united these two souls and it's on you now to nurture this relationship above all.

""Happy is the moment, when we sit together, with two
forms, two faces, yet one soul you and I"
-- RUMI"

CHAPTER FIFTY-THREE

THE PILLAR OF TRUE LOVE

My husband is an Engineer by profession, I love him for his steady nature, and I love the warm feeling when I lean against his broad shoulders.

Three years of courtship and now, two years into marriage, I would have to admit, that I am getting tired of it. The reasons for me loving him before have now transformed into the cause of all my restlessness.

I am a sentimental woman and extremely sensitive when it comes to a relationship and my feelings, I yearn for the romantic moments, like a little girl yearning for candy. My husband is my complete opposite, his lack of sensitivity and the inability of bringing romantic moments into our marriage has disheartened me about love.

One day, I finally decided to tell him my decision, that I wanted a divorce.

"Why?" he asked, shocked. "I am tired, there are no reasons for everything in the world!" I answered. He kept silent the whole night and seems to be in deep thought with a lighted cigarette at all times. My feeling of disappointment only increased, here was a man who can't even express his predicament, what else can I hope from him? And finally, he asked me:" What can I do to change your mind?"

Somebody said it right, it's hard to change a person's personality, and I guess, I have started losing faith in him. Looking deep into his eyes I slowly answered: "Here is the question, if you can answer and convince my heart, I will change my mind, Let's say, I want a flower located on the face of a mountain cliff, and we both are sure that picking the flower will cause your death, will you do it for me?" He said:" I will give you your answer tomorrow...." My hopes just sank after listening to his response.

I woke up the next morning to find him gone, and saw a piece of paper with his scratchy handwriting, underneath a milk glass, on the dining table near the front door, that goes.... My dear, "I would not pick that flower for you, but please allow me to explain the reasons further.." This first line was already breaking my heart. I continued reading.

"When you use the computer you always mess up the Software programs, and you cry in front of the screen, I have to save my fingers so that I can help to restore the programs. You always leave the house keys behind, thus I have to save my legs to rush home to open the door for you. You love travelling but always lose your way in a new city, I have to save my eyes to show you the way. You always have the cramps whenever your "good friend" approaches every month, I have to save my palms so that I can calm the cramps in your tummy.

You like to stay indoors, and I worry that you will be infected by infantile autism. I have to save my mouth to tell you jokes and stories to cure your boredom. You always stare at the computer, and that will do nothing good for your eyes, I have to save my eyes so that when we grow old, I can help to clip your nails, and help to remove those annoying white hairs. So I can also hold your hand while strolling down the beach, as you enjoy the sunshine and the beautiful sand... and tell you the colour of flowers, just like the colour of the glow on your young face... Thus, my dear, unless I am sure that there is someone who loves you more than I do... I could not pick that flower yet, and die.. "

My tears fell on the letter, and blurred the ink of his handwriting... as I continue reading... "Now, that you have finished reading my answer, if you are satisfied, please open the front door for I am standing outside bringing your favourite bread and fresh milk... I rush to pull open the door, and saw his anxious face, clutching tightly with his hands, the milk bottle and loaf of bread....

Now I am very sure that no one will ever love me as much as he does, and I have decided to leave the flower alone...

That's life and love. When one is surrounded by love, the feeling of excitement fades away, and one tends to ignore the true love that lies in between peace and dullness.

Love shows up in all forms, even very small and cheeky forms, it has never been a model, it could be the most dull and boring form.. . flowers, and romantic moments are only used and appear on the surface of the relationship. Under all this, the pillar of true love stands... and that's our life... Love, not words win arguments...

CHAPTER FIFTY-FOUR

THE THREAD OF RELATIONSHIPS

After the death of a jeweller, his family was in grave trouble. They did not have enough money even for food. One day, his wife gave her son a sapphire necklace and said - "Son, take this to your uncle's shop. Ask him to sell it and give us some money."

The son took that necklace and reached his uncle's shop. His uncle looked at the necklace thoroughly and said - "Son, tell your mother that the market is very slow right now. If she sells it after some time, she will get a good price." He gave him some money, and further said, "come and sit with me at the shop from tomorrow."

So, the next day onwards, the boy started going to the shop every day, and there he started learning how to test diamonds and gems.

Soon, he became a well-known connoisseur of diamonds. People started coming from far and wide to get their diamonds tested.

One day his uncle said, "Son, bring that necklace from your mother now...tell her that the market is good now, and you will get a good price."

Taking the necklace from his mother, the young man tested it himself and found that it was a fake. He began to wonder why his uncle was such a great connoisseur...why didn't he inform them?

Leaving the necklace at home, he returned to the shop.

Uncle asked, "Didn't you bring the necklace?" He said, "Uncle, it's artificial... But why did you hide this from me?"

Then his uncle said, "If I had told you it was fake when you had first brought the necklace to me, you would have thought that I was only doing it because you were in a difficult situation.

Today when you yourself have the knowledge, you know for sure that the necklace really is fake. At that time, it was more important for me to take care of the relations than to speak the truth."

The truth is that without knowing everything we think, see and know in this world is wrong. And because of this, our relationships become a victim of misunderstandings which then lead to rifts, and our life starts falling apart.

The invisible thread by which relationships are tied is nourished by love and trust.

"Don't leave someone's side at the slightest strain in relations...

It takes a lifetime to make people your own."

FINAL CONSUMPTION

HOW DO WE PLAN TO GET 'CONSUMED' FINALLY?

Many times I get overwhelmed just by looking at the platter of food that's placed before me for any meal.

A typical Indian platter would contain some vegetables, daal, rotis and rice and some sweets or fruit.

As I close my eyes to convey gratitude to all those who have made it possible for the food on this platter, tears would roll down many a time, just by trying to comprehend what all efforts have gone for this food for a duration of almost a year. Being a son of a farmer, I know what it takes for a hot roti to be

served on my plate.

The farmer during the summer, in the burning sun, prepares the field and the soil, awaiting the monsoons. He patiently waits for the monsoons. He has his seeds prepared. At the right moment after the rain, assembling the labours, bullocks and the equipment he sows the wheat or the jowar seeds. He then patiently waits for them to germinate. Then he takes care of the young crop by providing nutrition and removing the weeds. As the harvest time arrives, he is worried about the attack of thousands of birds. He somehow manages to protect the crop. He harvests the crop. That's a herculean task itself. He then has to sell it at the right price.

Once it's sold, it reaches the shop from where we purchased it, passing through various intermediaries.

When we buy the jowar, it's cleaned, and taken to the chakki for grinding. Thereafter hot water at the right temperature is mixed to make the right dough. From that dough jowar roti is prepared. To learn the skill of making jowar roti is task by itself. It takes months of training. This journey is applicable to all the dishes served on the platter, to be finally consumed by us.

Similar is the case with our clothes, our home where we live and the vehicle we travel in. We are the final consumers.

And to reach to the state of final consumption from the raw state, there's a mind-boggling journey. And when we introspect our own journey as human beings, the journey is even more mind-boggling. Pre - historians estimate our journey to a few thousand years of evolution.

In spiritual terms, the journey is of eighty-four lacs lives, to be in the present human life. Actually, we can transform this life into a life of the final state. Like the food on the platter, is in the final state. It has been prepared after a year-long process for final consumption. (Thereafter it goes back to the zero states, to the earth for recycling.)

Yes.

We are actually in that final state now. We can decide and act for ensuring our own FINAL CONSUMPTION. We have travelled for thousands of years and millions of lives, getting evolved at each stage - as the final product now.

The FINAL CONSUMPTION is the natural conclusion of our journey.

And that can happen by removing the layers of ignorance accumulated for many many lives. And that's not a difficult process. By AWARENESS of your own self, one can slowly help himself in the FINAL CONSUMPTION.

CHAPTER FIFTY-SIX

HABITS

A man was deeply troubled by the bad habits that were developing in his son. Whenever he would ask or explain to the son to leave the habit, he would get only one answer, "What is my age now, now are the days to live my life. Don't worry, gradually I will give up this habit. But he never tries to give up the habit. Father was worried about it.

A saint used to live in his village, that man respected that saint very much and used to take advice from him in difficult times of his life.

He went and narrated all his agony to the saint, the saint listened to him patiently and said, "Okay, bring your son to me tomorrow morning, I will talk to the child!

The next morning the father and son reached the saint.

The saint said to the son, "Let us both take a walk in the garden." And he slowly started moving forward.

While walking, the saint suddenly stopped and said to the son, "Can you uproot this plant?"

"Yes, what is the big deal in this.", and saying so, the son easily uprooted the plant and looked at the saint with pride. The saint smiled.

Then they went ahead and after a while, the saint pointed to a slightly bigger plant and said, "Can you uproot it too?" And looked at the child with questioning eyes.

As if the son was enjoying all this, he immediately started uprooting the plant. This time he took some hard work, but after a lot of effort, he uprooted it too. With the pride of winning back, he smiled seeing the saint, the saint was also smiling.

They went ahead again and after some time again Mahatma Ji, pointing towards a gudah tree, asked the son to uproot it.

The son grabbed the trunk of the tree and started pulling it vigorously. But the tree was not even taking its name to move. Because his torso was thin in appearance, but the roots of the hibiscus were deep inside. The boy was not giving up because of pride, but when the tree did not budge even after trying a lot, the son said, "Hey! It is so strong that it is impossible to uproot it.

The embarrassment of defeat was now on his face.

The saint smiled, explaining to him lovingly and said, "Son, the way you have experienced small plants and this tree today, the same happens with our bad habits, nature, and our desires, when they are new, It is easy to leave, but as they grow old, their roots become very strong, and they take their roots deep in the form of nature, lust, then it becomes very difficult to leave them.

The son understood the point of the saint and he decided to give up bad habits today itself.

CHAPTER FIFTY-SEVEN

INNOCENCE VS MATURITY

Remembering the innocent carrier of life let one take back into flashbacks of childhood memories. Not to me but to those who are now reading this post. One of the commons among all is running of nose and having the taste of that leaked yellow liquid known as cerebrospinal fluid rhinorrhea.The liquid is clear, without any odour. It has the consistency of drinking water. The healthy bloom in cheeks gave one an aura of innocence. The irritation revealed when one sponge, press and twist them and kiss them on such soft and smooth cheeks, leads to crying. Yes, it happens with all. Don't forget the screaming for not going to school when our parents hold us in their nap and forcefully let us go to school. the playing of housekeeping games and dreaming of a wedding at innocent age always reflect one to laugh at. No one knows how the period of innocence pass off in struggling with books and exams, one attains Maturity at one stage.

While attaining Maturity one tries to Act as if one attained all world power in his/her hand. Tries to dominate and forget all childhood steps. But the Maturity in humans is not so easy to accomplish or achieve. One have to go through many hurdles and lessons. Even after accomplish the age of the Maturity one act like the childish behavior.Runs after many illusion immaterial things of this materialistic world and tries to impress upon others with his/her inability. Every thing which comes have to go, Our life is like a running water and it never stops.

The real Maturity is to to surrender yourself completely and accept HIS will. The suffering caused by anyone do not repent and instead pray and give best wishes to them. The more we give positive energy , the positive thoughts will automatically elaborate from us. ...

CHAPTER FIFTY-EIGHT

EMOTIVE MORAL

The little boy came from school on Saturday and told his father, my teacher has given us homework to Hug 10 people and tell them - "Be patient, trust life and I Love you".

The Dad said - "OK, we will go to the Mall tomorrow morning and do it".

The child woke up all spirited up in the morning and got ready. Went to his Dad and said - "let's go!!"

The father said - "there is Heavy rainfall, I fear nobody might be there".

The Child still insisted. So the Father drove in the horrible rainy weather to the Mall.

They stood in the mall for 1 hour, and the little boy hugged 9 people.

His father then said - "now lets go, its raining heavily and we shouldn't get stuck!"

Sad the son went along with his father's orders. As they where driving past, the child pointed at a random house. Said - "please dad, just 1 person is remaining, I will go to that house and complete my homework"!

The father smiled and pulled the car over.

The child went to the door and began to ring the bell and pound the door strongly with his knuckles. He kept waiting. Finally, the door was opened gently.

A lady came out with a very sad look and gently asked:

"What can I do for you, son?

With radiant eyes and a bright smile the child said:

"Ma'am my teacher has told me to Hug 10 people and tell them - "Be patient, trust life and I Love you".

I have hugged 9. May I hug you and pass the message to you?

The Lady embraced him and started crying profusely.

On seeing that the Boy's father came out of the car. He went to the lady and asked - "Any problem madam?"

She composed herself, took them inside, gave them a cup of tea and then told his father -

"My husband died a while ago leaving me totally alone in this world. Today morning the loneliness took over me. Since morning I have been thinking that this is the end of the road for me.

Then I took a chair and a rope to my bedroom and decided to end my life. As I was seeing the world for one last time, I begged for forgiveness to GOD and then heard this knock. I thought to leave it. But then nobody comes to visit me.

When I opened the door, I couldn't believe what my eyes saw this little child. And when he said, "Be patient, trust life and I Love you".

I knew it was a message from God.

Suddenly I realized I don't want to die anymore, and decided to make something productive of my life.

REMEMBER - Give positive thoughts to people.

Tell them you stand by them.

And even if nothing, just listen to them

CHAPTER FIFTY-NINE

CHARACTER ASSASSINATION

One mistake you should never make in life, is to allow yourself to be recruited by someone, to hate another person who hasn't wronged you.

Hear this: "We must avoid taking hasty conclusion because of what others are saying about someone else..."

What people say about others, says a lot about them. I am repeating this more directly: The things you say about others, says a lot about you! I can tell a lot about a person by what they choose to see in others.

Character assassination is a pervasive and destructive phenomenon that is found everywhere.

You find it in families, places of worship, organizations, work places, etc.

Character assassination is the deliberate, malicious, unjustified and sustained effort to damage the reputation or credibility of an individual.

Character assassination is the slandering of a person usually with the intention of destroying public confidence in that person.

"Character Assassination" is the act of lowering one's character in a bid to ruin the character of others.

There are people that take maximum delight in ruining other's reputation. These set of people have what I will like to call 'Destructive Tendencies'. They oil their own ego by pulling other people down. PhD(pull him down).

False allegations are the most chronic form of mental abuse. When people can't kill your dreams and purpose, they will try to assassinate your character. There are some people that your spirit will always irritate their demons! Once they realize hating isn't working they start telling and spreading lies about you. People are assassinated once but 'Character Assassination' kills daily! Character assassination is a form of emotional violence against others.

Someone once said, "A friend of my enemy is my enemy." One of the things that hinders us from living a fulfilling and inclusive life is bringing past bias and sentiments into present relationships. A friend of your enemy is not necessarily your enemy; it all depends on intentions and contributions. God can use your enemy's friend to bless you!`

CHAPTER SIXTY

SEVEN CRITICAL 'DON'TS' THAT YOU REALLY NEED TO GUARD YOURSELF AGAINST

Refusing to getting trapped in them will help you live a more productive, fulfilling and unbiased life. They are:

1. Don't conclude about people because of what others say about them: Never draw up conclusions based on what others tell you about someone. It is a lack of social intelligence that makes people draw conclusions on others based on what other people say about them. I know you've heard about emotional and financial intelligence, but there is something called social intelligence. This is the kind of intelligence that keeps you sane even when others are trying to pollute your mind against someone else until you have thoroughly confirmed the veracity of the claims before you. Judges are trained to have this kind of intelligence in order to avoid biased judgments.

2. Don't inherit other people's enemy: It is total lack of education and enlightenment when you automatically make your friend's enemies your own. Don't make people your enemies just because they are not in good terms with your friends.

3. Don't use your children as weapons of war: God can use your enemies to bless your children Stop using them to fight those you don't like. Your children will need to discern their enemies for themselves; never use your parental influence to make your children hate others. You may often need to guard them with their choice of friends but never plant the seed of discord in the heart of your children against someone else.

4. Don't gang up with others to hate someone: Don't join the majority to hate someone – you may realize that the person has no offence. Someone said, "If you don't see it with your own eyes, or hear it with your own ears. Don't invent it with your small mind and share it with your big mouth". Never join the multitude to hate someone else.

5. Don't be used as a weapon in other people's battles: It is not every battle that you must involve yourself in. Refuse to be used as weapons in other people's battles. When people fight dirty, refuse to take sides. Observe deeply before concluding finally.

6. Don't hate people just because they don't behave like you: That someone is not your tribe doesn't make them your enemy. It is a waste of education if the only people you like are those that are like you. The greatest proof of our education is in how we respond to people whose opinions are different from ours. People who think their opinions are superior to others are most prone to overestimating their relevant knowledge and ignoring chances to learn more.

The people who don't think like you are your greatest source of enlightenment. It is normally people that are not like us that help us grow the most. Companies that had maximized growth are really those that value diversity and inclusion.

7. Don't judge people until you know the whole story: Someone once said, "Beware of the half-truth. You may have gotten hold of the wrong half". Don't judge other people's choices without understanding their reasons.

If people say something bad about you or judge you as if they know you, don't easily get affected. Remember this, dogs bark if they don't know the person. People who are intimidated by you talk about you with hopes that others won't find you so appealing.

Stay away from people who talk bad about others daily; these kinds of people carry a negative spirit, and a negative spirit is contagious. The real problem is not that they are unhappy with others, but they are unhappy with themselves.

Stop the destructive habit of talking about people behind their back. Talking badly about someone else while they aren't there to defend themselves says more about you than the person you're talking about. When you have issues with people, try and discuss it with them. Stop discussing it with others. Someone once said, "Don't talk about me until you have talked to me". Stop spreading false information and rumours about others.

Rumours are carried by haters, spread by fools and accepted by idiots! Stop creating walls of contention, rather help build bridges of understanding among people.

CHAPTER SIXTY-ONE

YOUR LIFE BELONGS TO YOU

During a robbery in Guangzhou, China, the bank robber shouted to everyone in the bank: "Don't move. The money belongs to the State. Your life belongs to you."

Everyone in the bank laid down quietly. This is called "Mind Changing Concept" Changing the conventional way of thinking.

When a lady lay on the table provocatively, the robber shouted at her: "Please be civilized! This is a robbery and not a rape!"

This is called "Being Professional" Focus only on what you are trained to do!

When the bank robbers returned home, the younger robber (MBA-trained) told the older robber (who has only completed Year 6 in primary school): "Big brother, let's count how much we got."

The older robber rebutted and said: "You are very stupid. There is so much money it will take us a long time to count. Tonight, the TV news will tell us how much we robbed from the bank!"

This is called "Experience." Nowadays, experience is more important than paper qualifications!

After the robbers had left, the bank manager told the bank supervisor to call the police quickly. But the supervisor said to him: "Wait! Let us take out $10 million from the bank for ourselves and add it to the $70 million that we have previously embezzled from the bank".

This is called "Swim with the tide." Converting an unfavorable situation to your advantage!

The supervisor says: "It will be good if there is a robbery every month."

This is called "Killing Boredom." Personal Happiness is more important than your job.

The next day, the TV news reported that $100 million was taken from the bank. The robbers counted and counted and counted, but they could only count $20 million. The robbers were very angry and complained: "We risked our lives and only took $20 million. The bank manager took $80 million with a snap of his fingers. It looks like it is better to be educated than to be a thief!"

This is called "Knowledge is worth as much as gold!"

The bank manager was smiling and happy because his losses in the share market are now covered by this robbery.

This is called "Seizing the opportunity." Daring to take risks!

So who are the real robbers here?

CHAPTER SIXTY-TWO

LIFE AS A RIVER

The River as a metaphor for life is not a new concept. As long as philosophers have pondered the deepest mysteries of the Universe, many comparisons have been made between life and the fickle current of a river. The River is as constant as it is inconsistent, ever-changing. The same river can be slow or fast, deep or shallow, loud or silent, wide or narrow, churning and white or green and flat as glass.

A river is a river, always there, and yet the water flowing through it is never the same water and is never still. It's always changing and is always on the move. And over time the river itself changes too. It widens and deepens as it rubs and scours, gnaws and kneads, eats and bores its way through the land.

It is this constant, ever-changing nature that makes The River a classic metaphor for all of life's journeys. On the water, the current determines what is needed from us at any given time. When approaching a rapid, The River demands our attention, forces us to plan our route, to set up for the run and have the physical strength to keep our course. When the water is still, we are allowed to rest and enjoy the scenery, or prepare for the next rapid. All the wishing, fighting, crying and demanding in the world will not change the river's current...we must accept it for what it is, choose our course and do our best.

Rivers never flow in a straight line - they crisscross the landscape and find the best path to reach their destination. Similarly, as professionals and entrepreneurs, we also need to be prepared to navigate through life's challenges and stay the coarse until we reach our goals. Enrich and Persevere like a River. Rivers flow hundreds and thousands of miles, and nourish the land along the way. The land becomes richer because of the river flowing by it. We can do the same by making a positive impact on the people we come across everyday.

Rivers do not fight and rush for the sake of fighting and rushing. They push, pull, erode, and rip apart their surroundings, not for its own sake, but to achieve the serenity and peace which we often associate with the river. This is a valuable life lesson from which we can learn. In our daily lives, are we struggling for the sake of the struggle, or so that the end goal can be achieved?

CHAPTER SIXTY-THREE

STOCKHOLM SYNDROME

Do you remember the film 'Darr' where Shahrukh Khan is a charmer but eventually turns out to be a psychopath? Juhi Chawla was saved but there are women who even after knowing that their charmer is a psychopath continue to be possessed by the love they feel for the cheat. It's such a complex emotional symbiotic relationship that it beats logic too. This is called Stockholm Syndrome where the captive turns against the law and protects the captor or abuser.

Meenu is married, has two grown-up children but was possibly missing romance and passion in her life. When there is deep desire the mind wishes to fill it up by hook or crook. So now in walks the charmer, let's name him Mohan. Meenu and Mohan chat on the social networking platform and he insists they meet. Initially, Meenu resists but then as these stories go, she meets him.

Meenu takes into his sob stories regarding his luck with his finances, victimized by his wife and laden with profitable ideas which no one wants.

Meenu decides to help him and slowly falls into the quicksand that begins to swallow her. She rents a place for him to open a restaurant, furnishes his rented apartment, buys him smart clothes and even a car. Meenu's husband has no idea where his bank balance is dwindling. Meenu is not asked about this aberration as there has been an awkward silence between them for a long time.

Mohan after a few months let's Meenu know about his wife and son living in South India. He speaks of the strained relationship to gain sympathy from Meenu. As time goes by Meenu's emotional involvement scares Mohan and so he decides to vanish from the city. He leaves without a trace with Meenu having to pay debts he owes. Meenu is devastated and feels she needs answers to this betrayal.

The CBI contacted Meenu and she found out that this man was a murderer and had killed his second wife. He was married four times and Meenu realized her folly regarding trusting the cheater. Mohan had fled but now Meenu was wanting to know why she was unable to read the man's intentions and fell into a trap.

Past Life Experience:

Meenu visualized herself in a tribal dress with a beaded skirt and long black hair. She lived in a big ornamental house and the year was 1928.

The first figure that appeared was a man with a long silken robe who was her father (current life husband). He was authoritative but loving.

The next scene is of her standing on a cliff and waiting for someone. The next figure who appears is a man whom she loves (This man resembled Mohan).

Trauma: The father kills the lover because he suspects his intentions.

The young woman lives in grief after the loss of her lover. The father is distraught seeing his daughter in this manner and feels his action was unwarranted. Guilt is the most dangerous emotion as it robs the mind of all rationale.

Insight: She realized that Mohan came into her life for a short time to hurt both her and her husband. Also what made her husband help her through this difficult period and what is making him help her even meet Mohan in the Nasik prison to seek answers so that she can be at peace.

Complex relationships are really difficult to unravel. I was surprised to hear Meenu say," If Mohan's jail term is ten years I am willing to wait for him." Deep guilt, love, and betrayal are like poison, it corrodes the very essence of the person and fills it with deep suffering.

If you have such a toxic relationship, remember to use logic, rationale, and inner soul voice to step away from it.

CHAPTER SIXTY-FOUR

YOU DEFINE YOUR OWN LIFE

*"You define your own life. Don't let other people write your
script.*
    --OPRAH WINFREY"

This quote means that you are the captain of your ship and sometimes you have to steer that ship through stormy seas until you complete your journey and are in a safe harbor. You don't let anyone or anything lead you off course.

You stay firmly at the helm until your journey is a success. You're responsible for your crew and the passengers and you may have to ride tumultuous waves to get them home. In business, your crew and your passengers are your employees and your customers. As captain, you have a duty to them. Honor over profit. Honesty over short-term gain. Passion for others over greed.

To put it differently, we can even say that, When writing the story of your life, don't let anyone else hold the pen.

The other key meaning I take from this is, literally, don't let anyone else write your story. You know as a unique individual who you are and what you contribute to the world. You know that you're an inherently decent person. You know what's in your heart. Always make sure that the truth comes out and don't allow other individuals with different motives and agendas of their own to misrepresent who you are or what you have done.

It's a sad fact of life that there will be occasions when people put their own spin on events and it doesn't represent reality. That's why you have to always speak up for yourself. If you don't, you can't expect anyone else to. Don't let inaccuracies or untruths become common perception. Speak up and stand up for yourself. Don't let them take the pen away from you.

You have to wield the pen and write the chapters of your life both in terms of the actions that you take and how they are recorded in your own history.

Tell yourself that you want to ride. Also say that you will. Because It's time to start something.

So, start your chapter and make sure you're writing each word with passion.

CHAPTER SIXTY-FIVE

LAO TZU'S ENLIGHTENMENT

He said: I was sitting under a tree and I had done all that could be done, all that was humanly possible and I was completely frustrated. Much had happened through it, but not all; something was lacking, missing, and the missing link was the most difficult to find, elusive.

Then while I was sitting under a tree, a leaf, a dry leaf, fell from the tree slowly, and moved in the wind. The wind was going north, the leaf moved north; then the wind changed course, started moving towards the south, and the leaf started moving towards the south; then the wind stopped — and the leaf fell down on the earth, with not a single complaint, with no struggle on its own part, with no direction of its own.

If the wind was going south, it was going south, if the wind was going north, it was going north, if the wind stopped, it fell down on the earth and rested beautifully.

Then again there was some wind and again it rose high in the sky — but there was no problem. Suddenly I understood, the message hit home. From that day I became a dry leaf and the missing link which was so elusive was elusive no more. The missing link was only this: that you can attain many things through effort but you cannot attain Tao through effort.

Finally you have to leave effort — and suddenly everything fits, you are in accordance. Then you don't give direction, then you are no longer a director; then you don't say to the winds: Go south, because I am on a journey towards the south. Then you don't have any destination; then the destiny of the whole is your destiny; then you are not separate.

Then you don't think in terms of individuality, you have become part of the whole and wherever the whole is going you are going. If the whole changes its mind, you change your mind; if the whole stops the journey, it is beautiful; if the whole runs, you run with it. That is what 'in accordance' means.

With not a bit of mind of your own, when you have become a no-mind, the whole lives through you, lives you, moves through you, moves you. Now you don't breathe, the whole breathes you. Then everything is a benediction, a blessing. How can you be tense then? Worried about what? All worries exist because you have brought an individual destiny into your mind against the destiny of the whole — you are moving up-current.

This is the whole secret of your failure — you are moving up-current. Then you are worried, tense, in anguish, in anxiety, almost going mad — anybody will go mad if they are going up-current because the fight is so hard and so meaningless. And one day you will feel tired and then it will look like a frustration, a failure. The wise man leaves this up-current nonsense, he simply allows the river to take him wheresoever it is going. If it is going anywhere, good; if it is not going anywhere, good — then suddenly you are still, silent.

Only then, never before, does real meditation happen and all effort is dropped. But you have to make the effort first, otherwise you will never understand that it has to be dropped. You can drop it only if you have been in it — and from the very beginning it is almost impossible for you to be so wise as to drop it. How can you drop a thing which you don't have?

CHAPTER SIXTY-SIX

DIE EMPTY

The most beautiful book for a young man to read is *"Die Empty" by Todd Henry.*

The author was inspired and got this idea of writing this book while attending a business meeting.

When the director asked the audience: "Where is the richest land in the world, a person in the audience answered "Oil-rich Gulf states."

Another added: "Diamond mines in Africa."

Then the director said: "No it is the cemetery. Yes, it is the richest land in the world, because millions of people have departed and they carried many valuable ideas that did not come to light nor benefit others. It is all in the cemetery where they are buried."

Inspired by this answer, Todd Henry wrote his book, "Die empty" where he did his best to motivate people to pour out their ideas and potential energies in their communities and turn them into something useful before it is too late.

The most beautiful of what he said in his book is: *"Do not go to your grave and carry inside you the best that you have. Always choose to die empty."*

The true meaning of this expression is to die empty of all the goodness that is within you. Deliver it to the world, before you leave.

One life to live.

One life to die.

One life to learn and practice what you have learnt.

One life to learn multiple skills, arts, hobbies, sports, multiple professions.

One life to experience joy in what you perform.

One life to share, give, pass on, teach and donate so that you die empty but Rich every which way.

You have a limited number of days on Earth. This book sends an urgent message: make them count!"

"If you have an idea, perform it.

If you have knowledge, give it out.

If you have a goal, achieve it.

CHAPTER SIXTY-SEVEN

DO YOUR DREAMS SCARE YOU?

""If your dreams do not scare you, they are not big enough."*
ELLEN JOHNSON SIRLEAF
(Africa's first woman president)"

The size of your dreams must always exceed your current capacity to achieve them. If your dreams don't scare you, they aren't big enough."

If you think about the achievements of some of the world's most famous or successful people, it all started for them with a dream. Surely, their dreams scared them. But that didn't stop them. It fueled them.

At the very heart of any successful person's goal, is a plan. That plan needs to be acted upon on a daily basis, and not simply set and forgotten about.

Do Your Dreams Scare You? What do you want out of life? What do you want to achieve or become? What ideals do you want your life to represent? What value do you want to add to society?

The mind is the most powerful tool. It can be razor sharp when focused, helping to attract good things into our lives. But it can also work against us as a deterrent, focusing on negativity and seeing only problems, thus begetting more problems.

Wherever you point your mind, that's the direction that your life is going to move in. So be excruciatingly careful about what you focus on. That's also precisely why your dreams should scare you. Because, no matter what your dreams are, it's purely an element of focus. You might as well focus on something really big rather than something minute, since whatever you focus on, you'll move towards.

Everything comes in time to those who can wait. It's just a matter of time. You never actually know how close you are if you give up. And while there isn't a single success formula or recipe for everyone, at the heart of making those dreams that scare you come to fruition, is persistence.

This should remind us to stop playing small. We weren't put on this earth to be average or good. We were put here to be great. Set your intentions and goals really high, to stretch yourself to growth. Every monumental success was seemingly impossible at one point.

Having a dream means that there is something in your mind that you wish could turn into reality. If you really want your dreams to come true, you need to try and explore them.

We often hold ourselves back because we are either afraid or don't trust our capabilities. If we don't try, we put an end to every possibility, but if we give it a go, even if we are unable to achieve what we want, we open other doors of opportunities that we might not have known previously. We meet people, create new connections and learn new skills that can all guide us on the path to success.

If you want to achieve something, always give it a try. You won't lose by trying, but you possibly would gain another opportunity in life.

CHAPTER SIXTY-EIGHT

A HEAD FULL OF FEARS HAS NO ROOM FOR DREAMS

Dreams at their very Nature remind us of our passions and deepest desires. In other words, they tell us who we are and who we strive to be.

we often push our dreams to the side to take a backseat to fears and anxieties. Those dreams that once defined us and gave us a beautiful and unique identity get replaced by a cloud of negativity and doubt.

Dreams are like our life's magnet. It pulls us to places, and becomes one of the driving forces for our life. our dreams develop our passion, purpose, and our faith. So what happens when we give more place to our fears than our dreams?

Fears create a forcefield that block opportunities from getting toward us, because our fears stop our forward motion. The things that were once flying towards our life become blocked by fears. Listening to our fears slows us down and keeps us away from actualizing our dream.

When we dream and believe that our dream can be actualized, we live in a state of expectation.

The longer you stay in a state of expectation, the more opportunities are presented your way. This is why lending your time towards dreaming and expecting is far more valuable than living in a state of fear. Let's change the way we think and speak, let's remove fear from our minds, hearts and words.

CHAPTER SIXTY-NINE

SALT VS RICE

If you were to cook 3 cups of rice, would you add 3 cups of salt to it?

Certainly not!

So, in every preparation of rice, the grains of rice always outnumber the salt, yet a little salt makes a huge difference/impact in the overall outcome.

In the room in which you currently are, look up at the ceiling...

What is the size of the bulb compared to the size of the room? It is probably a ratio of 1:5000.

Yet, darkness flees the entire space once the small bulb is flipped on.

If I am the salt of the earth, and the light of the world, then "little me" has the ability to make big things happen..

Sometimes, because we feel outnumbered or overwhelmed at the sheer magnitude of evil or wrong-doers, we then choose powerlessness, and decide to go with the flow, not standing up for what we believe is right.

Little doesn't mean insignificant.

You are significant. Your presence should make a BIG difference. Stop waiting to be on the side of the majority. They may be the majority, but they are the trivial majority, and you are the impactful minority.

They are the rice of the world, and you are the salt of the world..

They are the room and you are the light.

Make your influence felt!

Remember:

You are the world's seasoning, to make it beautiful...

So if we can just do the right seasoning to make even one life beautiful our life is worth living.

Onwards and Upwards! Be the salt in someone's life today

CHAPTER SEVENTY

SHIPS DON'T SINK...

Ships don't sink because of the water around them; ships sink because of the water that gets in them. Don't let what's happening around you get inside you and weigh you down.

No matter who you are or where you came from, we all have to overcome adversity. Success is not determined by how skilled you are in avoiding challenges but how you let it mold you once you face them. Will you let adversity break your will or use it to strengthen your confidence and skills?

There is a dangerous delusion from which many people unsuspectingly suffer. It is the belief that we feel the way we feel and make the choices we make because of what happens to us. When we have this dangerous belief, we put the power over us into the hands of luck, strangers, the whims of the world. It is like having a hole in your ship, inviting the world in and asking them to sink you.

Life is going to happen how ever way it happens, for you. But you can control the outcome of how you emotional react to any situation. It takes practice and the motivation to get back up. Some times sadness is the proper reaction to a situation. But for how long? The more you can be above your emotional reaction, the better you can understand. Letting emotion control you doesn't actually fix your problems. So in the end why let the difficult people or situations or circumstances consume you.

Don't let what is happening around you get inside you and weigh you down. Start with an important affirmation: What I do today is important because I am exchanging a day of my life for it. When tomorrow comes, today will be gone forever, leaving in its place something that you have left behind. Allow it be something that got you closer to your highest good.

CHAPTER SEVENTY-ONE

VICTORY

Does our victory depend only on our talent?

After winning several archery competitions, a young bowman began to consider himself the greatest archer. Wherever he went, he would challenge people to compete with him and after defeating them, would make fun of them.

Once, he decided to challenge a famous master and reached his monastery among the mountains early in the morning. "Master, I challenge you to an archery contest," said the young man. The master accepted the young man's challenge. The competition began.

In his first attempt itself, the young man hit the distant target right in the middle, and in the next attempt, he pierced the first arrow that had hit the target. Proud of his ability, the young man said, "Tell me Master, can you do better than this? If 'yes' then do it, if 'no' then give up."

The master said, "Son, come after me!" The master walked and reached near a dangerous ditch. The young man got a little nervous seeing all this and said, "Master, where are you taking me?"

The master said, "Don't worry son, we are almost there, we just have to go to the middle of this wrecked bridge."

The young man saw that someone had built a makeshift wooden bridge to connect the two hills and the master was asking to go over the same. The master reached the middle of the bridge, took out an

arrow from the arch and aimed it precisely at a tree trunk in the distance.

After aiming, the master said, "Come son, now you also prove your efficiency by aiming at the same tree."

The young man moved forward fearfully and with great difficulty reached the middle of the bridge and somehow shot an arrow, but it did not even land anywhere near the target. The young man was disappointed and accepted his defeat.

Then the master said, "Son, you have mastered the bow and arrow, but you still do not have control over the mind, which is very important to be able to hit the target in any situation.

Son, always keep in mind that as long as a person has a desire to learn, his knowledge keeps increasing...but as soon as he has the ego of being the best, from then on his downfall starts."

The young man understood what the master was saying. He realized that his knowledge of archery works only in favorable circumstances and that he still had much to learn; he immediately apologized to the Master for his arrogance and vowed to always learn like a disciple and not boast of his knowledge.

Friends, we too can be physically strong, we can have many talents as well, but if our heart is not ready to accept every situation, can we lead a successful life? Ego is not to be used to hurt others. It is to keep pointing the finger back towards myself saying, "Okay, I can do it better than I did last time."

CHAPTER SEVENTY-TWO

ASSOCIATION

The rain drop from the sky: If it is caught in hands, it is pure enough for drinking. If it falls in a gutter, its value drops so much that it can't be used even for washing the feet. If it falls on hot surface, it perishes.

If it falls on lotus leaf, it shines like a pearl and Finally, if it falls on oyster, it becomes a pearl. The drop is same, but its existence & worth depend on whom it associates with.

Always be associated with people who are good at heart.

We are so influenced by the people we surround ourselves with. It's nearly impossible to rise to your own personal greatness if you aren't surrounding yourself with people who are doing the same.

One of the most important decisions we make in life is who we choose to be around. In fact, there is an old proverb that reads, "Show me your friends and I'll tell you who you are." Quite often we become like the people we're around. Based on that, we must be cautious about whom we surround ourselves with because of the short- and long-term implications. One of the most important decisions we make in life is who we choose to be around. In fact, there is an old proverb that reads, "Show me your friends and I'll tell you who you are." Quite often we become like the people we're around. Based on that, we must be cautious about whom we surround ourselves with because of the short- and long-term implications. Sometimes we have to make hard choices about what to eliminate in order to dedicate time to the relationships.

Surround yourself with positive people. Hold them close. They will give you energy and help you create the career success you deserve."

Successful people surround themselves with positive people – people who are both positive by nature, and positive about their life and career success. Positive people are optimistic; and optimism is the first step in building your self-confidence and life and success.

CHAPTER SEVENTY-THREE

FAMOUS SPEECHES - MARTIN LUTHER KING

""Hatred paralyseslife;love releases it. Hatred confuses life; love harmonizes it. Hatred darkens life; love illuminates it"

--Dr. Martin Luther King Jr "

We must discover the power of love, the power, the redemptive power of love. And when we discover that we will be able to make of this old world a new world. We will be able to make men better. Love is the only way --Dr. Martin Luther King Jr

Just as Darkness cannot drive out darkness; only light can do that, Hate cannot drive out hate; only love can do that. Hatred paralyzes life; love releases it. Hatred confuses life; love harmonizes it. Hatred darkens life; love illuminates it.

In one of his famous speeches Martin Luther King said, **I'm concerned about a better World.**

I'm concerned about justice;
I'm concerned about brotherhood and sisterhood;
I'm concerned about truth.
And when one is concerned about that, he can never advocate violence.

For through violence you may murder a murderer, but you can't murder murder. Through violence you may murder a liar, but you can't establish truth. Through violence you may murder a hater, but you can't murder hate through violence. Darkness cannot put out darkness; only light can do that.

And I say to you, I have also decided to stick with love, for I know that love is ultimately the only answer to humankind's problems. And I'm going to talk about it everywhere I go. I know it isn't popular to talk about it in some circles today. And I'm not talking about emotional bosh when I talk about love; I'm talking about a strong, demanding love. For I have seen too much hate, and I say to myself that hate is too great a burden to bear. I have decided to love. If you are seeking the highest good, I think you can find it through love. And the beautiful thing is that we aren't moving wrong when we do it, because John was right, God is love. He who hates does not know God, but he who loves has the key that unlocks the door to the meaning of ultimate reality.

It's usually harder to choose to love than to allow yourself to hate. Remember that it'll do you more good. And it gets easier if you work to make it a habit. Hatred produces nothing but an endless cycle of violence. As long as hate is met with further hate, there is never any hope of the cycle of hate and violence coming to an end. The only hope for ending hatred and violence is to break the cycle by injecting love and forgiveness into the cycle.

CHAPTER SEVENTY-FOUR

BE GRATEFUL

Count your blessings, by noticing the many gifts you regularly receive, is a good way to commence a daily practice, and start to shine a light on gratitude in daily life.

The tiniest creatures of God,

Even the insects have a sense of gratefulness!

An ant was caught on a dry leaf that was being carried down a flooded river and it called out from its tiny heart to God for succour.

Promptly a kite that was flying over the river, dove and rose up, with the leaf on its beak; for the bird mistook the leaf for a fish or frog!

The bird was sorely disappointed, but, the ant was delighted to land on hard ground!

"God came as a kite and rescued me, it felt. I must be grateful to the bird, to all birds," it resolved.

One day, while on its morning round, the ant saw a hunter aim an arrow at a bird;

The Ant bit the heel of the hunter, just when he was releasing the mortal shaft; the aim failed; the bird flew off, and was saved.

Do whatever you can for whoever you can, in the 'Pay it forward' circle of life.

God sends us his blessings through various means and different forms.

The 'miracles' in your life are the results of someone's prayers and good deeds.

Be grateful for your blessings, for all the 'miracles' in your life and stay blessed forever.

CHAPTER SEVENTY-FIVE

A PRECIOUS HUMAN LIFE

If you know your life is precious, and you only have one to live, it's only wise to invest it in something that you are passionate about because the only way to do great work is to do what you love.

So sit down, think for a moment, ask yourself, what do you want to invest this your precious life into?

For that moment, let go of the fear of what people will say, remember it's your life not theirs.

You must discover what your passion is because if your heart is not in something, you will never give your best, and if you don't give your best, you will never be great.

If you are not passionate about what you do, you will waste your life, in the end, all you will have is regrets.

If you don't invest your life in something worthwhile, you will throw it away on nothing that won't worth in a while.

The passion was given to you by God for a reason, and giving it everything you got is the best way to live. For when passion drives you, nothing can stop you.

CHAPTER SEVENTY-SIX

THE LAW OF LEAST EFFORT

" " Accept People Situations and events as they occur. Take responsibility for your situation and for all events seen as problems. Relinquish the need to defend your point of view."
--- Deepak Chopra "

The fourth spiritual law of success expounded by Deepak Chopra is 'the Law of Least Effort.'
This law is based on the fact that nature's intelligence functions with effortless ease and abandoned carefree.

This is the principle of least action, of no resistance. This is, therefore, the principle of harmony and love.
When we learn this lesson from nature, we easily fulfill our desires.

If you observe nature at work, you will see that least effort is expended.
Grass doesn't try to grow, it just grows.
Fish don't try to swim, they just swim.
Flowers don't try to bloom, they bloom.
Birds don't try to fly, they fly. This is their intrinsic nature.

The earth doesn't try to spin on its own axis; it is the nature of the earth to spin with dizzying speed and to hurtle through space.

It is the nature of babies to be in bliss.
It is the nature of the Sun to shine.
It is the nature of the stars to glitter and sparkle.
And it is human nature to make our dreams manifest into physical form, easily and effortlessly.

In Vedic Science, this principle is known as the principle of economy of effort, or "do less and accomplish more." Ultimately you come to the state where you do nothing and accomplish everything. This means that there is just a faint idea, and then the manifestation of the idea comes about effortlessly. What is commonly called a "miracle" is actually an expression of the Law of Least Effort.

Nature's intelligence functions effortlessly, frictionlessly, spontaneously. It is non-linear; it is intuitive, holistic, and nourishing. And when you are in harmony with nature, when you are established in the knowledge of your true Self, you can make use of the 'Law of Least Effort.'

Least effort is expended when your actions are motivated by love, because nature is held together by the energy of love. When you seek power and control over other people, you waste energy. Let's try & make use of the 'Law of Least Effort'

CHAPTER SEVENTY-SEVEN

FREE YOURSELF FROM THE PRISON OF YOUR MIND

Most of us interpret life-based on events we have experienced in the past. While memories help us to maintain a sense of continuity in life, it can also hold us captive as we use them to build walls around us, imprisoning our minds and seeing life only through a small tinted window.

The result is, that we perceive reality through memories from the past and worries about the future, creating a distorted version of reality. So we need to think about how we can pull down our prison walls and set ourselves free. The answer is surprisingly simple. Be present at this moment. Because now is where reality is. The present moment is the only thing you have got now. The past is gone and will never come back. The future is elusive and is beyond anyone's grasp. Whatever you can do now happens at this moment.

When you surrender completely to now and put all your attention on every moment, your full awareness connects you to the flow of life. That is when living becomes effortless and intuitive. You will begin to respond to each moment instinctively without worries or anxieties.

Actions inspired by full awareness will no longer be driven by fears, angers, anxieties or stress. Even in the face of great difficulties, instead of dwelling in a state of bitterness, self-pity or cynicism, full awareness gives you the ability to focus on choices that bring happiness to you as well as others. And that is the taste of true freedom.

CHAPTER SEVENTY-EIGHT

WELCOME CUP OF TEA

A group of 15 soldiers led by a Major were on their way to the post in the Himalayas where they would be deployed for the next 3 months. The batch who would be relieved waited anxiously. It was cold winter & intermittent snowfall made the treacherous climb more difficult. If someone could offer a cup of tea. . the Major thought, knowing it was a futile wish.

They continued for an hour before they came across a dilapidated structure, which looked like a tea shop but was locked. It was late at night. "No tea boys, bad luck", said the Major. But he suggested all take some rest there as they have been walking for 3 hours. "Sir, this is a tea shop and we can make tea... We will have to break the lock", suggested one soldier. The officer was in great dilemma to the unethical suggestion but the thought of a steaming cup of tea for the tired soldiers made him give the permission. They were in luck, the place had everything needed to make tea and also packets of biscuits. The soldiers had tea & biscuits and were ready for the remaining journey. The major thought, they had broken open the lock and had tea & biscuits without the permission of the owner. They're not a band of thieves but disciplined soldiers. He took out an Rs1000/- note from his wallet, placed it on the counter, and pressed it under the sugar container so that the owner can see it. The officer was now relieved of his guilt. He ordered to put the shutter down and proceed.

Three months passed, and they continued to do gallantly in their work and were lucky not to lose anyone from the group in the intense insurgency situation. It was time for another team to replace them. Soon they were on their way back and stopped at the same tea shop which was open and the owner was present in the shop. The owner an old man with meagre resources was very happy to greet 15 customers. All of them had tea and biscuits. They talked to the old man about his life and experience especially about selling tea in such a remote place.

The old man had many stories to tell, replete with his faith in God. "Oh, Baba, if God is there, why should He keep you in such poverty ?", commented one of them. "Do not say like that Sahib! God actually is there, I got proof 3 months ago." "I was going through very tough times because my only son had been severely beaten by the enemy who wanted some information from him which he did not have. I had closed my shop to take my son to the hospital. Some medicines were to be purchased and I had no money. No one would give me a loan for fear of the terrorists. There was no hope, Sahib". "And that day Sahib, I prayed to God for help. And Sahib, God walked into my shop that day." "When I returned to my shop, I found the lock broken, I felt I was finished, I lost whatever little I had. But then I saw that God had left Rs 1000/= under the sugar pot. I can't tell you Sahib what that money was worth that day. God exists Sahib. He does."

The faith in his eyes was unflinching. Fifteen pairs of eyes met the eyes of the officer and read the order in his eyes clear and unambiguous, "Keep quiet". The officer got up and paid the bill. He hugged the old man and said, "Yes Baba, I know God does exist. And yes, the tea was wonderful." The 15 pairs of eyes did not miss to notice the moisture building up in the eyes of their officer, a rare sight. The truth is "YOU" can be GOD to anyone.

CHAPTER SEVENTY-NINE

LOOK FOR THE GOOD

"What we see depends mainly on what we look for
-- JOHN LUBBOCK"

In the Mahabharata the preceptor, Dronacharya, while explaining an important life lesson to his pupils, asked the eldest of the Pandavas, Yudhishtra and the Kauravas, Duryodhana, to go round the kingdom and find out how many good persons and bad persons were there.

Yudhishtra came back and reported that he could not find a single bad person. He could find some negatives only in himself.

Duryodhana came back and told the Guru that he could not find a single good person. If there was any good man, it was only him, he said.

All the students in the ashram were perplexed by the outcome. They asked, Guru Dronacharya, how come Duryodhana could not find a good person and Yudhisthira could not find a bad person.

Guru Dronacharya then calmly told his students that what we are internally we see that in the world.

Duryodhana was filled with pride, jealousy and desire and therefore he was unable to find a good person. Yudhisthira was filled with piety, humility, peace and goodness and therefore he was unable to find a bad person in the same country.

What matters is our outlook if we have a positive outlook we will be able to see light even in the darkest corner of the cave.

Everything thus depends on our outlook and not on the nature of the things we observe.

If you look at the world with a good mind everything will appear good.

There is nothing wrong with Srishti (CREATION),

Just change your Drishti (VISION)!

If you look for the good, you will only find the good and if you look for the evil in everyone, you will only find the bad.

Look for only the good in Everyone.

CHAPTER EIGHTY

AN INSPIRING ROMANTIC STORY

I was 12 years old when I got married to him. I still remember. He came with a horse cart to marry me. No one got married in my entire village with a horse cart. I was so happy and proud! My husband paid 10 takas at that time for it. He could have bought a very big paddy field with that money!

After our wedding, my husband used to call me 'Ranga Bou' which means 'beautiful wife'. He said I was the most beautiful woman he had ever seen in his whole life. But my husband had such dark skin colour that the village people always made jokes about him. They used to tell him he was like "a black stone wearing a pearl necklace." But my husband never minded; he seemed happy and smiled when people told that joke! He always said to me, "See how beautiful you are!" For the last 75 years, we have been together. Two years ago, I went to visit my elder

son and his family. I left my husband with my younger son and his family. My daughter-in-law said he used to call out every 10 minutes, "where is my Ranga Bou! Has she called? When she is coming back?" He becomes crazy without me. We have never been separated in our entire married life. We wake up together and pray our morning prayers together. He cannot eat if I don't cook the meal with my own hands! But when we sit down to eat he gives me the biggest piece of the fish!

If I ever got mad at him and stopped talking to him, he always sat beside me and never moved anywhere else until I smiled at him. If I disappeared for a few minutes from his sight, he used to look for me everywhere and started calling, "where is my Ranga Bou?" I can never go anywhere because of him.

Maybe we will not see each other much longer. We are almost near our last age! I don't want to go before him. He will become crazy without me. He will look for his Ranga Bou everywhere! My wish is for God to take me after him! - Mosir Uddin Sarder (105) and his Ranga Bou 87 ...

CHAPTER EIGHTY-ONE

THE 90/10 PRINCIPLE - STEPHEN COVEY

I am sharing this article I came across written by Stephen Covey. I hope you enjoy it

Discover the 90/10 Principle

It will change your life (at least the way you react to situations) What is this principle? 10% of life is made up of what happens to you 90% of life is decided by how you react What does this mean? We really have no control over 10% of what happens to us -

We cannot stop the car from breaking down. The plane will be arriving late, which throws our whole schedule off. A driver may cut us off in traffic We have no control over this 10%

The other 90% is different, You determine the other 90%

How? ....By your reaction You cannot control a red light but you can control your reaction. Don't let people fool you; YOU can control how you react.

Let's use an example

You are eating breakfast with your family, Your daughter knocks over a cup of coffee onto your business shirt. You have no control over what just happened. What happens next will be determined by how you react.

You curse, You harshly scold your daughter for knocking the cup over, She breaks down in tears. After scolding her, you turn to your spouse and criticize her for placing the cup too close to the edge of the table. A short verbal battle follows.

You storm upstairs and change your shirt. Back downstairs, you find your daughter has been too busy crying to finish breakfast and could not get ready for school. She misses the bus.

Your spouse must leave immediately for work. You rush to the car and drive your daughter to school Because you are late, you drive 40 miles an hour at a 30 mph speed limit.After a 15-minute delay and throwing a $60 traffic fine away, you arrive at school.Your daughter runs into the building without saying goodbye.

After arriving at the office 20 minutes late, you find you forgot your briefcase Your day has started terrible As it continues, it seems to get worse and worse. You look forward to coming home. When you arrive home, you find a small wedge in your relationship with your spouse and daughter Why?

Because of how you reacted in the morning. Why did you have a bad day?

A) Did the coffee cause it

B) Did your daughter cause it

C) Did the policeman cause it

D) Did you cause it

The answer is "D"

You had no control over what happened with the coffee. How you reacted in those 5 seconds is what caused your bad day.

Here is what could have and should have happened
Coffee splashes over you, Your daughter is about to cry. You gently say, "It's ok honey, you just need to be more careful next time"

Grabbing a towel you rush upstairs, After wearing a new shirt and with your briefcase, you come back
down in time to look through the window and see your child getting on the bus, She turns and waves.

You arrive 5 minutes early and cheerfully greet the staff. Your boss comments on how good the day you are having

Notice the difference

Two different scenarios

Both started the same

Both ended different

Why?

Because of how you **REACTED**

You really do not have any control over 10% of what happens

The other 90% was determined by your reaction

Here are some ways to apply the 90/10 principle

If someone says something negative about you, don't be a sponge. Let the attack roll off like water on glass

You don't have to let the negative comment affect you. React properly and it will not ruin your day

A wrong reaction could result in losing a friend or dear one /being fired/getting stressed out etc

How do you react if someone cuts you off in traffic

Do you lose your temper?

Pound on the steering wheel?

Do you curse?

Does your blood pressure skyrocket?

Do you try and bump them?

WHO CARES if you arrive ten seconds later at work?

Why let the cars ruin your drive?
Remember the 90/10 principle, and do not worry about it

The 90-10 principle is incredible. Very few know and apply this principle. The result? Millions of people are suffering from undeserved stress, trials, problems and heartache.We all must understand and apply

"Life is 10% of what happens to you, and 90% of How you react to it"

CHAPTER EIGHTY-TWO

THE TREASURES THAT WE SEARCH, ARE ALL WITHIN US

This is a story of a person that lived under a tree leading a life mostly of misery and adversity. He would beg for a living and sometimes even had to sleep hungry. He had to endure all kinds of rough weather. Sometimes he would also have some happy moments when some of his friends came to visit him but then they would depart and again he would be alone by himself. One day the man got sick and passed away.

Wanting to pay their last respects some of his close friends decided to bury him under the very tree where he used to live. As soon as they started digging their axe hit a hard box. As they dug some more they found a big box of treasure. It was full of gold and precious gems. The friends who found the treasure became richer than their wildest imagination. Unfortunately, the poor man passed away living his entire life in misery without ever knowing about the treasure that lay a few feet under him. Imagine if he would have known about this treasure while he was alive. Even a fraction of that treasure could have removed his misery.

This story although sad has a mystical and deeper message for all of us. Upon deeper introspection we will realize we are that person. We live in this world abound with pain and misery. We also have some fun along the way with our possessions and attachments but still it is all nothing but illusion. Nothing stays with us, all things leave us. The treasure buried right under us is our own consciousness or Atma. That treasure is enough to secure for us perpetual happiness and liberation. For those of us that are still alive and breathing, it is not too late to shift our focus towards securing this treasure. Once we find this treasure we can forever terminate the cycles of life and death. We will experience perpetual bliss.

The digging required for this treasure is leading a spiritual life with the tools of selfless service, Satsang, good company, devotion, meditation and reading scriptures etc. This treasure is buried deep within us only and we already have all the resources to secure it. May our Guru and God inspire us to secure this treasure in this very life.

CHAPTER EIGHTY-THREE

ANYTHING THAT COSTS YOU YOUR PEACE IS TOO EXPENSIVE

We all have needs that venture beyond work and tests, money and grades. We have things, people and places that make us feel at peace. It may be some trivial things like the beach in the early morning sun and reading the pages of a novel we have or spending time with our loved ones... These needs are what make us feel whole. Peace and fulfilment go hand in hand.

We as humans have an innate desire for happiness and at the top of all our desires is the word peace or contentment. The reason is that one can be at Peace in adversity or undesirable times. One can be at Peace even with the loss of a loved one, with the right kind of mindset or attitude. When we reduce our desires for material things or draining relationships, we automatically start attracting peace of mind.

Give up the things that cause you stress. Give up the things that keep you up at night. Cultivate the things that make you actually happy. Enjoy the moments of peace that get scarcer and scarcer as we get older. Spend your time wisely, don't funnel all your cash into things that don't make you a richer and more content person because of it. Making a conscious decision to do so is extremely important, change your priorities to suit what you really want. The stresses of life can wait. They can. You don't actually have to prioritise financial gain or work progression if those things do not make you feel happy. If what makes you happy is doing things that create memories that you'll look back on, do it! And just quickly I'm not saying that you should quit your job and become a nomad trekking all over the world(unless you want to), but just adjust your perspective. Just don't put your personal happiness aside to create that ideal life that isn't concurrent with what you want from your life. It's a way too high a cost.

CHAPTER EIGHTY-FOUR

ENJOY THE COMPANY OF YOUR CHILDREN

A beautiful post ....from one mother to another mother

There were days when My home used to be filled with laughter, arguments, fights, jokes and loads of mischief.

Pens and books all over, and clothes messing the rooms, thrown on the beds.

I used to shout at them to tidy up their mess.

In the morning:

One will wake up and say :

Mama, I can't find a certain book.

And the other will say: I can't find my perfume,

And one will say Mama where's my homework?

And another: Mama I forgot to complete my homework.

Everyone used to ask about their lost possessions. And I will say, but take care of your stuff, be responsible, you have to grow up.

And today I stand at the doorway of the room. The beds are empty. All the cupboards have only a few pieces of clothes in them. And what remains is the smell of perfume that lingers in the air.

Everyone had a special smell. So I take in the smell of their perfume for maybe it will fill the empty ache in my heart.

All I have now is the memory of their laughs and their mischief and their warm hugs.

Today my house is clean and organized and everything is in its place, and it is calm and peaceful. But it is like a desert with no life in it. Do not become angry with your kids about the mess.

Every time they come to visit and they spend time with us when they are ready to leave. They pull their bags and it is as if they tug my heart along with them.

They close the door behind them and then I stand still and think of the many times I shouted at them to close the doors.

Here I am today, closing my own doors. Nobody opens it besides me. Each one has gone to a different city or a different country. All are left to find their own path in life.

They have grown up and I wished that they could stay with me forever.

Oh! God..... Take care of them & all other children wherever they may be, for You are their guide and protector ...and always keep them happy.

If your children are still in the stage that you need to talk and talk before they could get things done in the house, please, cherish and endure it with joy, don't nag, they will soon leave your home for you, remember they were not there at the beginning of your marriage. Now that they are around, make them happy.

Dedicated to all mothers and fathers.

CHAPTER EIGHTY-FIVE

WHEN LIFE GETS TOUGH, WHICH ONE ARE YOU?

Once upon a time, a daughter complained to her father that her life was miserable and that she didn't know how she was going to make it.

She was tired of fighting and struggling all the time. It seemed that just as one problem was solved, another one soon followed.

Her father, a chef, took her to the kitchen. He filled three pots with water and placed each on a high fire. Once the three pots began to boil, he placed potatoes in one pot, eggs in the second pot, and ground coffee beans in the third pot.

He then let them sit and boil, without saying a word to his daughter. The daughter moaned and impatiently waited, wondering what he was doing.

After twenty minutes he turned off the burners. He took the potatoes out of the pot and placed them in a bowl. He pulled the eggs out and placed them in a bowl.

He then ladled the coffee out and placed it in a cup. Turning to her he asked. "Daughter, what do you see?"

"Potatoes, eggs, and coffee," she hastily replied.

"Look closer," he said, "and touch the potatoes." She did and noted that they were soft. He then asked her to take an egg and break it.

After pulling off the shell, she observed the hard-boiled egg. Finally, he asked her to sip the coffee. Its rich aroma brought a smile to her face.

"Father, what does this mean?" she asked.

He then explained that the potatoes, the eggs and coffee beans had each faced the same adversity– the boiling water.

However, each one reacted differently.

The potato went in strong, hard, and unrelenting, but in boiling water, it became soft and weak.

The egg was fragile, with the thin outer shell protecting its liquid interior until it was put in the boiling water. Then the inside of the egg became hard.

However, the ground coffee beans were unique. After they were exposed to the boiling water, they changed the water and created something new.

"Which are you," he asked his daughter. "When adversity knocks on your door, how do you respond? Are you a potato, an egg, or a coffee bean? "

Moral: *In life, things happen around us, and things happen to us, but the only thing that truly matters is what happens within us.*

CHAPTER EIGHTY-SIX

10 TOP LESSONS FROM THE BOOK "MAKE YOUR BED"

1. Start Your Day With a Task Completed

Lesson number one is to start the day by ticking off a straightforward task, such as making our beds. This simple act of making your bed gives you hope, and symbolizes your discipline and determination to get better.

2. No Person is an Island

No matter how independent you are, the truth is that you can't go it alone. All of us experience life's tough times, but we shouldn't feel like we need to navigate them by ourselves.

3. Accept That Life's Not Fair

Sometimes life isn't fair or reasonable. We don't have to like this reality, but we have to accept it, and know that we only cause ourselves more suffering if we stay on the blame train. We can either complain or take the hit and carry on.

4. What Doesn't Kill You Will Only Make You Stronger

Failure makes us stronger. It's a hard truth that no matter how hard we try, we'll all face failure at some stage. However, we don't have to fear failure, or feel defeated by it.

5. Dare Greatly

Have you ever jumped headfirst into anything? If we always play it safe and continuously try to mitigate potential struggle, humiliation, or failure, we will find it hard to reach our potential.

6. Make Courage Your Friend

When we're most scared, we need to find the courage to help us surmount obstacles to achieve our goals. When life throws us with what often feels like insurmountable challenges: Hold onto courage and keep swimming.

7. Rise to the Occasion

It's often the darkest moments that reveal our most profound strength. It's always worth remembering that there will be moments in life where our spirit feels crushed, and It's these moments that call on us to search for the best in us.

8. Give People Hope

Hope is something that a lot of us cling on to. We can also inspire hope and be strong for others. McRaven says, "If you want to change the world, start singing when you're up to your neck in the mud."

9. Never, Ever Quit

And, never ever quit. If you want to change the world, don't ever, ever ring the bell. If you do quit, you'll regret it for the rest of your life.

10. True Leaders Must Learn From Their Failures

True leaders must learn from their failures, use the lessons to motivate themselves, and not be afraid to try again or make the next tough decision.

This book will make you a disciplined individual.
A must-read book

CHAPTER EIGHTY-SEVEN

POSITIVE OUTLOOK

When lobsters win a fight (e.g. to compete for their territory), it changes their biology.

Winning lobsters experience a boost of serotonin, which makes them more "proud" and they stand taller.

By contrast, their weaker counterparts have less serotonin, remain timid and curl up out of fear & are most likely to be defeated by the tall, confident lobsters in the next fight.

This reinforces the pecking order of lobsters.

Similarly, humans often mimic this behaviour too. Our hierarchies are determined by our behaviours.

People who frequently "win" in life become emboldened by their winning streak.

Their confidence allows them to face new challenges head-on. And their previous wins fuel their cycle of success.

Whereas people who constantly feel like life is never in their favour, often hunch and slouch around life.

They are more risk-averse. And they tend to approach each situation as if they know they're going to fail. Over time, it becomes a self-fulfilling prophecy, reinforcing their negative outlook on life.

So, if you are trying to get ahead in life, think like a winning lobster. Pay more attention to your posture and how you stand. Have a positive outlook.

Even if you are not in a winning situation, having an upright posture exudes dominance and confidence. Always strike your winning pose.

Your posture matters more than you think — it's not just about how the world sees you, but how you see yourself.

Encourage the serotonin to flow plentifully through the neural pathways desperate for its calming influence.

Always, always have a positive outlook and stay blessed forever.

YOUR MIND IS A MAGNET

Think of yourself as a human magnet, constantly attracting what you speak, think and feel.

We magnetically attract circumstances, events and people that are in harmony with our dominant thoughts, emotions and patterns of self talk. This means that what we think about most of the time, how we think about things, talk to ourselves, and the emotions we experience throughout our days, determine the events, circumstances, and people that we tend to attract into our lives.

We also magnetically attract into our lives that which we talk about most of the time. This not only includes how we talk to ourselves but also encapsulates how we talk to others, how we talk about our circumstances and our life experience as we go about our day.

The law states that you are the sculptor of your future and your ultimate life destiny; that you are the painter of your life's canvas and experience; and that you are the architect of your life circumstances and attitude. For better or worse, whether good or bad, the universe simply does not judge how we sculpt our lives, what paint we use on our canvas, or how we design our circumstances. It simply responds to the intentions of your creative mind by bringing forth into your life events, people and circumstances that correspond with your dominant patterns of thinking, talking and emotional longings.

It is important to remember that nothing can happen outside of you unless it is first created within you via your thoughts, emotions, self-talk, and beliefs. Therefore by transforming the inner aspects of your mind (the cause), you will gain ascendancy and control over the reality that is outside of you (the effect). Take Full Responsibility for Actions and Circumstances. Expect that Your Problems are Not Permanent.

The universal Law of Magnetic Attraction is a powerful and all-encompassing law that determines and dictates what we have or don't have in our lives. The law is neutral, and therefore how you use it rests completely in your conscious hands. So condition your mind to be a magnet that attracts only positivity in thoughts, words and action by not responding to negativity.

CHAPTER EIGHTY-NINE

A PERFECT MASTER

A man went in search of a Master. He was ready to go around the world, but he was determined to find the Master, the true Master, the Perfect Master.

Outside his village, he met an old man, a nice fellow sitting under a tree. He asked the old man, " Have you ever heard in your long life ... look like a wanderer ..."

He said, " Yes, I am a wanderer. I wandered all over the earth. "

The man said, " That is the right kind of person. Can you suggest to me where I should go? I want to be a disciple of a Perfect Master. "

The old man suggested a few addresses to him, and the young man thanked him and went on.

After thirty years of wandering around the earth and finding nobody who was exactly fulfilling his expectations, he came back dejected, and depressed. The moment he was entering his village he saw the old man who had become very old now, sitting under a tree. And suddenly he recognized that he is the Master! He fell at his feet and said, " Why didn't you say it to me, that you are the Master? "

The old man said, " But that was not the time for you. You could not recognize me. You needed some experience. Wandering around the earth has given you a certain maturity, a certain understanding. Now you see. The last time you met me, you had not seen me.

You had missed it. You were asking me about some Master. That was enough proof that you could not smell the fragrance. You were utterly blind; hence I gave you some bogus addresses so you could go.

But even to be with the wrong people is good, because that is ... how one learns. For thirty years I have been waiting for you here. I have not left this tree. "

In fact, the young man, who was not young anymore, looked at the tree and was even more surprised.

Because in his dreams, in his visions he was always seeing that tree and there was always a feeling that he would find the Master sitting under this tree.

Last time you had not seen the tree at all. The tree was there, the Master was there, EVERYthing was ready ... but HE was not ready."

- Sufi Story

CHAPTER NINETY

WHEN THE WIND BLOWS

Once there lived a farmer who owned land along the coast of the Atlantic ocean. Even after letting out several advertisements for recruitment to take care of his farm, no one seemed to sign up for it.

People were reluctant to work along the Atlantic, it had frequent raging storms. These storms were cruel, and violent and destroyed every building and crop field they touched.

After months of advertising and request refusals, a man approached the farmer for the job to take care of the farm.

"Do you have any skills or experience to work on a farm like this?" the farmer asked him.

"Well, I may not have enough experience, but I can sleep when the wind blows", replied the man.

Although the farmer wasn't much convinced by the man's answer, the farmer was too desperate to have someone to help him on the field that he hired him anyway. The man worked well around the farm. The farmer was pretty satisfied with the man.

Then one stormy night, the wind howled waking the farmer. The farmer immediately got off his bed, grabbed a lantern, and headed towards the quarter where his helper was sleeping.

"Wake up" the farmer yelled, throwing the soundly asleep man off the bed- " A storm is coming. Tie things down before they get blown away".

The man sat up and said- "No sir. I told you, I can sleep when the wind blows."

The farmer turned red with fury after listening to this. He controlled all his will to fire the man because at the moment it was more important to secure his fields and barn than to argue with his helper. The farmer ran out to tie the things up and was surprised by what he saw.

All of the haystacks were covered with tarpaulins. The chickens were in the coops, the cows were in the barn, the doors were closed and barred, and the shutters were firmly secured. Everything was tied down so that nothing could be blown away.

The farmer smiled as he comprehended what his employer said. Now, he understood what the man meant by when he said he could sleep when the wind blows. He went off to bed and slept soundly through the storm.

When you're prepared, physically, mentally, and spiritually, you have nothing to fear. Can you sleep when the wind blows through your life?

CHAPTER NINETY-ONE

THIS TOO SHALL PASS

There was a king, who once said to the court sages: "I have a ring with one of the finest diamonds in the world and I want to hide a message under the stone that can be useful in a situation of extreme despair. I will give this ring to my heirs and I want it to serve faithfully. Think of what kind of message will be there. It must be very short to fit in the ring."

The sages knew how to write treatises, but did not express themselves in one short sentence. They thought and thought, but did not come up with anything.

The king complained about the failure of his venture to a faithful old servant who raised him from infancy and was part of the family. And the old man said to him:

"I'm not a sage, I'm not educated, but I know such a message. For many years spent in the palace, I met a lot of people. And once I served a visiting mystic whom your father invited. And he gave me this message. I ask that you don't read it now. Save it under the stone and open it only when there's no way out at all."

The king listened to the old servant.

After some time, the enemies attacked the country and the king lost the war. He fled on his horse and his enemies pursued him. He was alone, his enemies were many. He rode to the end of the road. There was a huge deep cliff before him, if he fell there, it is the end. He could not go back, as the enemies were approaching. He already heard the clatter of their horses' hooves. He had no way out. He was in complete despair.

And then he remembered the ring. He opened it and found an inscription: ***"This too shall pass"***.

After reading the message, he felt that everything was quiet. Apparently, the pursuers got lost and proceeded in the wrong direction. Horses were no longer heard.

The king was filled with gratitude to the servant and the unknown mystic. The words were powerful. He closed the ring. And set out on the road. He gathered his army and returned to his state.

On the day when he returned to the palace, they arranged a magnificent meeting, a feast for the whole world - the people loved their king. The king was happy and proud.

An old servant came up to him and said softly: "Even at this moment, look at the message again."

The king said, "Now I am a winner, people are celebrating my return, I'm not in despair, not in a hopeless situation."

"Listen to this old servant," the servant answered. "The message works not only in moments when everything is bad but also in moments of victory."

The king opened the ring and read: "This too shall pass."

And again he felt a silence fall over him, although he was in the midst of a noisy dancing crowd. His pride dissolved. He understood the message. He was a wise man.

And then the old man said to the king; "Do you remember everything that happened to you? Nothing and no feeling is permanent. As night changes day, so moments of joy and despair replace each other. Accept them as the nature of things, as part of life".

Affirmation:

"Today I remember to love everything and everyone I come into contact with"

CHAPTER NINETY-TWO

THE IMAGINARY ROPE

A farmer was taking three of his donkeys for sale at the market.

On the way, he saw a river and decided to have a dip.

Since he had only two ropes to tie the donkeys to a tree, he looked around wondering how to tie the third one.

He saw a sage and sought his help if he could give him a rope to tie the third donkey. The sage did not have a rope but had a suggestion.

He told the farmer, "let the third donkey see you tying the other two donkeys to a tree. Then you pretend to tie this one also".

The farmer did as he was told and went for a dip in the river.

Coming back, he thanked the sage and saw that the donkeys stood exactly at the same spot where he had left them.

He untied the two donkeys and patted the third one to start moving.

Imagine his surprise when the third donkey stood still at the same spot.

Cajoling, kicking or talking did not help with the donkey, refusing to move from the spot.

The farmer went back to sage, who told him, "untie the third donkey".

"But", protested the farmer, "I have not tied him". The sage asked,

"You know it. But does the donkey know that?"

Sure enough, the farmer went back and pretended to untie the donkey.

The donkey moved immediately as though released and walked over to join the other two donkeys.

We are all like the third donkey, also tied up by too many imaginary ropes which are really non-existent.

The only truth is there are no boundaries in real life and anyone can stretch to any extent, and cross any limit.

Don't we all see records being broken, every time, everywhere and every day?

Our mind is a sacred enclosure into which nothing harmful can enter without our permission.

Hence as we go along this day, let us see what we can do with our minds.

Let's free the mind of limits, let's cut the imaginary ropes that tie us back & THINK BIG and stay blessed forever.

CHAPTER NINETY-THREE

CHANGE FOR THE BETTER

During the press conference to announce NOKIA being acquired by Microsoft,

Nokia CEO ended his speech by saying "we didn't do anything wrong, but somehow, we lost". Upon saying that, all his management team, himself included, shed tears sadly.

Nokia has been a respectable company. They didn't do anything wrong in their business, however, the world changed too fast. Their opponents were too powerful.

They missed out on learning, they missed out on changing, and thus they lost the opportunity at hand to make it big. Not only did they miss the opportunity to earn big money, but they also lost their chance of survival.

The message of this story is, that if you don't change, you shall be removed from the competition.

It's not wrong if you don't want to learn new things. However, if your thoughts and mindset cannot catch up with time, you will be eliminated.

The advantage you have yesterday will be replaced by the trends of tomorrow.

You don't have to do anything wrong, as long as your competitors catch the wave and do it RIGHT,

you can lose out and fail.

To change and improve yourself is giving yourself a second chance. To be forced by others to change is like being discarded.

Those who refuse to learn & improve, will definitely one day become redundant & not relevant to the industry. They will learn the lesson in a hard & expensive way!

Post-Covid, most people want to return to the Old normal, but let's ask yourselves,

"Do we want to return to the old normal where we were living in such a Fragile world, that a virus brought the world to a halt, to a lockdown? Where businesses are failing, countries are defaulting and as humans, we have not been able to raise a voice against the hunger and suffering of the needy, helpless and migrants and are not able to help them in their misery.

I shall rather prefer that we create and return to a better and more "Antifragile" world than the one we have left behind.

Change for the better & stay blessed forever.

CHAPTER NINETY-FOUR

WHATEVER EMOTION YOU INFUSE INTO THE WORLD, IT WILL FURTHER SPREAD

A 6 yr old boy was in the market with his 4 yr old sister. Suddenly the boy found that his sister was lagging behind. He stopped and looked back. His sister was standing in front of a toy shop and was watching something with great interest.

The boy went back to her and asked, "Do you want something ?" The sister pointed at the doll. The boy held her hand and like a responsible elder brother, gave that doll to her. The sister was very very happy...

The shopkeeper was watching everything and getting amused to see the mature behaviour of the boy...

Now the boy came to the counter and asked the shopkeeper, "What is the cost of this doll, Sir !"

The shopkeeper was a cool man and had experienced the odds of life. So he asked the boy with a lot of love & affection, "Well, What can you pay ?"

The boy took out all the shells that he had collected from the sea shore, from his pocket and gave them to the shopkeeper. The shopkeeper took the shells and started counting as if he were counting the currency. Then he looked at the boy. The boy asked him worriedly, "Is it less?"

The shopkeeper said," No, No... These are more than the cost. So I will return the remaining." Saying so, he kept only 4 shells with him and returned the remaining.

The boy very happily kept those shells back in his pocket and went away with his sister.

A servant in that shop got very surprised watching all these. He asked his master, "Sir! You gave away such a costly doll just for 4 shells ???"

The shopkeeper said with a smile, "Well, for us these are mere shells.

But for that boy, these shells are very precious. And at this age, he does not understand what money is, but when he will grow up, he definitely will. And when he would remember that he purchased a doll with the Shells instead of Money, he will remember me and think that the world is full of Good people.

It will help him develop a positive attitude and he too in turn will feel motivated to be Good."

Mind Mantra -

Whatever emotion you infuse into the world, it will further spread. If you do good, goodness will spread. If you do bad, negativity will spread.

Realize you are a very powerful source of energy.

Your good or bad will come back to you magnified. Not in the ways you want it, and probably not in the ways you can understand it. But it will come back.

CHAPTER NINETY-FIVE

A KNOT IN THE SHEET

At a school's parent meeting, the principal highlighted the support parents should give their children.

She understood that although most of the parents in the community were workers, they had to find some time to spend and spend with the children.

However, the principal was surprised when one of the parents got up and explained that he did not have time to talk to his son during the week.

When he left for work it was very early and his son was still sleeping when he returned from work it was very late and the boy was already lying down.

He also explained that he had to work that way to provide for the family's livelihood.

He also said that not having time for his son distressed him a lot and tried to replace that fault by giving him a kiss every night when he arrived at his house so that his son knew that he had gone to see him while he slept, he made a knot in the tip of the sheet.

When my son wakes up and sees the knot, he knows that his dad has been there and has kissed him. The knot is the medium of communication between us.

The principal was moved by that unique story and was even more surprised when she found that the son of that man was one of the best students in the school.

This fact makes us reflect on the many ways in which people can be present and communicate with others.

That father found his form, in a simple but efficient way. And the most important thing is that his son perceived through the knot, all his father's affection.

Sometimes we worry so much about the way we say the things we forget, the main thing is communication through feeling.

Simple details such as a kiss and a knot on the tip of a sheet, meant for that son, much more than a lot of empty gifts or apologies.

It is valid that we care about people, but the most important thing is that they know and can feel our concern and affection for them.

For communication to exist, it is necessary for people to "listen" to the language of our hearts, since feelings always speak louder than words.

It is for this reason that a kiss, covered with the purest affection, cures the headache, the blow of the knee or the fear of the dark.

Children may not understand the meaning of many words, but they know how to distinguish a gesture of affection and love, even if that gesture is only a knot in the sheet. A knot full of affection, tenderness and love.

"Live in such a way that when your children think of justice, love and integrity......They think of you"

CHAPTER NINETY-SIX

THE NUDGE THEORY

A father was cajoling his daughter to jump into the pool.

The little girl was adamantly refusing.

He was getting frustrated.

Then something happened.

He sweetened the offer with a promise of a big two-scoop Chocolate ice cream.

Splash!

She was in the water before he could count 3!

That little incentive was a nudge.

A nudge is a small act - an extrinsic one - that triggers people to change behaviours and take decisions.

The nudge theory is pretty popular worldwide and can be used in 3 forms:

Perception nudges

A food survey in the USA in 2012 revealed that people majorly opted for '99% fat-free' in place of '1% fat'!

It's a common perception psyche.

Motivation nudges

A municipal corporation in the UK was sending repeated emails to tax defaulters to pay up.

Without result, till it changed a tactic.

It sent a 'personalised' email to every defaulter with coloured graphics depicting details of taxpayers in the neighbourhood with no dues.

63% paid up in 3 days.

Ability nudges

In March 2009, the admin staff at the Schiphol Airport stuck up tiny fly-shaped stickers on the urinals in the men's washrooms.

It worked. Men aimed at the flies.

And 'spillages' were reduced by 80%.

Behavioural economist, Dr Richard Thaler, won the 2017 Nobel for his outstanding work on the Nudge theory in which he suggested consumer behaviour can be influenced by small suggestions and positive reinforcements.

Proponents of nudge theory suggest that well-placed 'nudges' can reduce market failure, save the government money, encourage desirable actions and help increase the efficiency of resource use.

A subtle suggestion may be more powerful than direct instructions.

Use the 'Nudge theory' to improve effectiveness & stay blessed forever.

CHAPTER NINETY-SEVEN

THE TRUE MEANING OF SILENCE

Four Monks Decided to Meditate Silently Without Speaking for Two Weeks.

They began with enthusiasm, observing a candle flame, and no one said a word the whole day. By nightfall of the first day, the candle began to flicker and then went out._

The First Monk blurted out, "Oh, No! The Candle Is Out."

The Second Monk Said, "Hey! We are Not Supposed to Speak!"

The Third Monk said in an Irritated Voice, "What Is This? Why Did You Two Break the Silence?"_

The Fourth Monk Smiled and said, "Wow! I'm the Only One Who Hasn't Spoken."

Reflections:

Each Monk Broke the Silence for a Different Reason, Each Of Which is a Common Stumbling Block in our Inner Journey: Distraction, Judgement, Anger and Pride.

The First Monk Got Distracted by One Aspect of his Experience (the Candle) and Forgot what was more Important - The Practice of Witnessing Without Reacting.

The Second Monk was more Worried About Others Following the Rules than Actually Practicing Himself. He was Quick to Judge Without Noticing that he Himself was Guilty of What he was Criticizing.

The Third Monk let his Anger Toward the First Two Monks Affect Him. The Singular Burst of Anger Ruined the Effort of the day.

The Fourth Monk Lost his Way Because of Pride. He Was Convinced he was Superior to the Others, Proving his Ignorance.

Why Did the Fourth Monk Speak At All?

He Could have Simply Maintained his Silence and he would have been successful in his Endeavor. But if he had, Chances are, the Other Three Might have Continued to Argue and Not Even Noticed his Silence.

Some people are like this. Their motto is "If I'm doing something good, but no one notices, I might as well not be doing it at all." They Believe that the Reward is Not in the Effort, But in the Recognition.

There is a beautiful quote, ***"It Is The Provence of Knowledge to Speak; it is the Privilege of Wisdom to Listen."***

As we learn to Truly Listen, Witness and Observe Without Impulsively Reacting with Distraction, Judgement, Anger and Pride, Then We Understand the True Meaning Of **SILENCE**

CHAPTER NINETY-EIGHT

WHAT IF THERE ARE NO MISTAKES? ONLY OPPORTUNITIES?

A thought-provoking story - even after a quick agreeing or disagreeing with what concluding views have been expressed, makes you ponder.

Five men got lost in a vast forest. They tried to find their way out.

The first man said, "I will follow my intuition and go left."

The second man said, "I will go right. I have a strong feeling about this."

The third man said, "I think I will walk back on the same path we came. This should be the safest option."

The fourth man said: "I think we are on the right track already, so I will keep going straight. I am sure this forest will end and I will find a village or a farm to ask for directions."

The fifth man said, "I don't know what to do. I think I will climb up this tall tree and take a better look around before I make up my mind."

So the fifth man did that. While he was climbing, the other four men scattered in their own directions. The fifth man now could see from above what was the shortest way to a village. He thought that the others should not have chosen the paths they did. He was wrong, though.

Each man chose his own path and gained a different experience. The man who went left found a long path but in the end, it led him to the town.

The man who went right had to fight a pack of wolves, but this way he learned how to survive in the forest.

The man who went back met another team of hikers and he made new friends.

The man who went straight found indeed a farm and was hosted by the family for a couple of days before leaving for the village.

Everyone was enriched in their own unique way by the journey.

Some reflections on this story...

What if, there are no "right" or "wrong" decisions?

Could it be that every decision offers us new experiences, which in turn offers us innumerable further opportunities for growth?

It has taken every decision of our life to bring us to where we are right now. In the fullness of the present, are we really in the wrong place? Even if it feels so, can we be sure?

What if there are no mistakes? Only opportunities?

CHAPTER NINETY-NINE

CARE OR CONTROL ?

Dr Hari was in consultation with a middle age couple. They started fighting right in front of him.

The upset husband said: 'See doc... I 'Care' so much for her and this is what I get in return. To which, the fuming wife replied: He doesn't care... he just 'Controls'..!

The care from one person was perceived as control by another!

This made Dr Hari think a lot...

What is the care and what is control?

How to identify them?

Soon he received the answer in his house itself.

He had an argument with his teenage daughter over a trivial discipline issue...

Harsh (though indirect) words were exchanged leaving both in tears...

After some time, as their emotions settled down, both said sorry to each other...

His daughter hugged him and said Papa, you know why you got upset? You were not upset because I did wrong... but you were upset because I did not follow your instructions..!

There is a big difference..!

He was stunned by her mature thinking pattern...

He received his answer too...

He was trying to control her under the disguise of care... that caused the conflict.

Moral

If you really 'care' for someone, you will not get upset or angry with that person. You will keep searching for different ways to help him or her.

If you are struggling in any relationship you need to closely observe if there is any subtle control hidden behind your apparent care...

Because Care is an expression of love while Control is an expression of ownership...

Control cuts...

Care connects...

Control hurts...

Care heals...

Keep caring for people but, do not control them...

Often people are not wrong... they are just 'different'...

Keep caring...

THE MAN IN THE ARENA

One of my favourite quotes is, **'Be an encourager. The world has plenty of critics already.' by Dave Willis.**

Whenever I think of that quote, I am reminded of a 110-year-old lecture by former US President Theodore Roosevelt.

I believe this passage provides a great perspective on the current times – The idea of empathising with those facing the action.

The lecture was titled **"Citizenship in a Republic"**, and this notable passage is referred to as "The Man in the Arena" and reads thus:

"It is not the critic who counts; not the man who points out how the strong man stumbles, or where the doer of deeds could have done them better. The credit belongs to the man who is actually in the arena, whose face is marred by dust and sweat and blood; who strives valiantly; who errs, who comes short again and again, because there is no effort without error and shortcoming; but who does actually strive to do the deeds; who knows great enthusiasms, the great devotions; who spends himself on a worthy cause; who at the best knows, in the end, the triumph of high achievement, and who at the worst, if he fails, at least fails while daring greatly, so that his place shall never be with those cold and timid souls who neither know victory nor defeat.

Someone who is heavily involved in a situation that requires skill, courage or tenacity – as opposed to someone sitting on the sidelines and watching – is referred to as **"the man in the arena."**

The 'correct Strategy' in hindsight or retrospect is easier, without a complete understanding of the circumstances or the context in which it was taken.

We are prone to criticizing, the govt officer, the entrepreneur, or that corporate manager whose decision-making skills we often criticize when they make a mistake or when his business is not doing well are all "Man in the arena."We are the ones sitting on the sidelines, watching, talking, and criticizing.

It is better to stumble than to do nothing or to sit by and criticize those that are "in the arena."

"The poorest way to face life is with a sneer," said Roosevelt in his speech. It is a sign of weakness; "To judge a man merely by success is an abhorrent wrong," he said.

Let's pause, Lets reflect, Let's respect, Lets empathise with and Salute the 'Man in the Arena' and stay blessed forever.

ZEN STORY: A GAME OF CHESS

A disillusioned young man travelled to a far-off monastery and approached the Master there.

"I am tired and disappointed with life. I seek enlightenment and freedom from all suffering. But I am not capable of endless meditation and austerities. If I tried that, I would revert to my bad ways and old life, despite knowing how painful it is. Is there a shortcut to enlightenment, Master?"

"Yes, there is," said the Master, "provided you are genuinely determined. What did you study in your youth? Is there anything, anything at all that you have really concentrated upon in your life?"

"Nothing much. I come from a wealthy family and never had to work. The only thing that's ever really interested me is chess. I used to spend a lot of time on the game."

The Master summoned his attendant. "Send Gyosei here; ask him to fetch a chess board when he comes."

"Sir, Gyosei cannot play chess."

"That's fine. Just call him."

When the monk Gyosei arrived, the Master arranged the chessmen on the board. He also asked for a sword and showed it to Gyosei. "Monk, you have sworn obedience to me and now, I am going to ask you for it. Play a game of chess with our visitor; if you lose, I shall chop your head off with this sword. If you win, I shall chop off our visitor's head." The look in the Master's eyes revealed that he would do exactly what he had said.

The game began. The young visitor felt sweat running down his back. He was playing for his life. He forgot his surroundings; the chessboard had become his world. Soon, when his opponent made a weak move, he launched a powerful attack. When Gyosei lost a pawn, the visitor stole a covert look at him. His was a face with intelligent eyes, lined with years of austerity and wonderfully serene. Even the prospect of death, it seemed, was not affecting him.

Gyosei made another faulty move. He was losing! The visitor, however, was overcome with reflections of his past life, worthless and devoid of meaning. He thought: "I cannot let this man die. If I die, the world loses nothing. I have wasted my time and achieved nothing. This monk has led a hardworking, disciplined life. His death will be a loss to the world." A wave of compassion arose within him. Deliberately, he made a wrong move, leaving his position open to attack.

Suddenly, the Master leaned forward and toppled the board over. The contestants stared at him. "There is neither winner nor loser here," declared the Master. He turned to the young man: "You only need two things to attain enlightenment – complete focus and compassion. Today, you have learned both. At first, you were entirely absorbed in the game. Out of that concentration arose compassion. It made you ready to sacrifice your life. Stay with us for some weeks, engage in our practices in the same spirit – your enlightenment is assured." The young man agreed and eventually attained his wish.

Lose yourself entirely in whatever you do. Compassion will naturally follow – it is concentration's faithful companion and cannot be practiced. This is the way to enlightenment.

CONTACT & CONNECTION

An old teacher was being interviewed by a young professional. The professional started interviewing the teacher as planned earlier.

Young professional: "Sir! In your last lecture, you told us about "Contact" & "Connection." It's really confusing. Can you explain?"

The old teacher smiled & apparently deviating from the question asked the young professional:

"Are you from this city?"

Professional: "Yeah!"

Teacher: "Who are there at home?"

The professional felt that the teacher was trying to avoid answering his question since this was a very personal & unwarranted question. Yet the young professional said: "Mother had expired. Father is there! Three brothers & one sister. All married!"

The old teacher, with a smile on his face, asked again: "Do you talk to your father?"

The young professional looked visibly annoyed...

The old teacher: "When did you talk to him last?"

The young professional, suppressing his annoyance said: "Maybe a month ago."

The old teacher: "Do your brothers & sisters meet often? When did you meet last as a family gathering?"

At this point, sweat appeared on the forehead of the young professional.

It seemed that the old teacher was interviewing the young professional.

With a sigh, the Journalist said: "We met last at a festival two years ago."

The old teacher: "How many days did you all stay together?"

The young professional (wiping the sweat on his brow) said: "Three days!"

Old teacher: "How much time did you spend with your Father, sitting right beside him?"

The young professional looked perplexed & embarrassed & started scribbling something on a paper...

The old teacher: "Did you have breakfast, lunch or dinner together? Did you ask how he was? Did you ask how his days are passing after your mother's death?"

Drops of tears started to flow from the eyes of the young professional.

The old teacher held the hand of the young professional & said: "Don't be embarrassed, upset or sad. I am sorry if I have hurt you unknowingly. But this is basically the answer to your question about "Contact & Connection!" You have 'Contact' with your father but you don't have a 'Connection' with him. You are not connected to him. Connection is between heart & heart!

Sitting together, sharing meals & caring for each other, touching, shaking hands, having eye contact, and spending some time together! All your brothers & sisters have

'Contact' but no 'Connection' with each other!"

The young professional wiped his eyes & said: "Thanks Sir for teaching me a fine & unforgettable lesson."

This is the reality today.

Whether at home or in society everybody has lots of contacts but there is no connection. Everybody is busy in his or her own world!

Let us not maintain just "Contacts" but let us remain "Connected!"

Caring, Sharing & Spending time with all our dear ones is the need of the hour.

TEMPTATION IS THE ROOT CAUSE OF UNHAPPINESS !

A beggar would chant God's name all day. One day, God manifested before the beggar and asked him to name his wish. The beggar wished for gold coins. God asked him, "What will you collect them in ?" The beggar put forward his sack. Before pouring gold coins into the sack, God said, "I will give you gold coins till you say 'enough', but on one condition. The gold coins should not fall to the ground. If they do, they will turn into dust". The beggar accepted the condition. Gold coins immediately started to rain into his sack. The sack began to fill up gradually, but the beggar could not control his avarice for gold. Now, with the weight of the coins, the sack began to burst at its seams. Despite realising this, the beggar did not say 'enough'. Finally, the inevitable happened; the sack tore open and all the coins fell to the ground and turned into dust! The beggar's discontentment lead to his downfall !

Where did the beggar go wrong? His greed made him discontented with the sackful of gold coins. By wishing for more, he lost everything and became unhappy. If you always want to be happy, then develop an attitude of contentment.

How to develop the attitude of contentment?

Do not fall prey to avarice; remember that the amenities you have are with God's grace and remain contented: 'Today, the needs of all the people are growing. They are introduced to new gadgets through the TV and feel like owning every single one! People want new clothes, shoes etc. even when they do not need them. If they are not given these things, many of them become unhappy. Sometimes, despite getting what they want, their desire to get the next best gadget continues.

At such times remember that the gadgets or amenities you have are due to God's grace; offer gratitude unto His Holy feet. This will keep your mind contented.

CONFIDENCE IS SILENT, INSECURITIES ARE LOUD

Some people feel the need to talk themselves up, to make themselves look better than they are. But without fail, these attempts to make their appearance more palatable say something louder than any tacky convertible: Please, please, please like me!

If you want to find the genuine ones look for the people hanging out in the background, calmly going about their business. These are people who know their value. Who know what they're good at and how. They're the people who do what needs to be done — not because somebody will praise them for it but because if they don't do it, nobody will.

In Philadelphia they tell a story about George Washington. When the first Continental Congress began the process of nominating the first President of the United States, many of the men present began talking about what a brilliant general George Washington had been. Rather than join into the conversation, Washington left the room. He didn't want or need to listen to the other people in the room sing his praises.

Knowing you're fantastic at something means your own approval is all you need. It's doubt that forces you to beg for somebody else to tell you how great you are.

Insecurities are louder than nearly anything else going on in our heads. They shout out the reason, the praise, the practical knowledge. Insecurity hovers over our accomplishments, asking, "Is this good enough? Tell me this is good enough!" Confidence, though, looks at an accomplishment and says, "Yeah, that's fine."

Be like George Washington and know how good you are. Know that you're killing it at life, at whatever it is you do, at being you, and leave it to other people to figure out how to handle all the amazingness you bring to the table.

BURIDAN'S DONKEY

Buridan donkey is a philosophical term or paradox that refers to a hypothetical situation where a hungry and thirsty donkey is placed exactly halfway between a pile of hay and a bucket of water.

Since his hunger is supposed to be equal to his thirst, the donkey is reluctant to eat and drink, and cannot choose either and prefer it at the expense of the other. In theory, it would die of both thirst and hunger as it would be unable to decide which one to get to first and he will not be able to make any rational decision between straw and water.

We all face similar situations many times in life and our inability to decide either way ends up with making us lose the opportunity.

The other night my wife asked me, "What do you want to have for dinner, Indian Food or Chinese food?"

It was a simple question, but I had a hard time answering it. In my head, Both cuisines had equal weight, and I had no plausible reason to choose one over the other.

The choice is perceived as freedom, but sometimes between a rock and a hard place, or between two roads—both well-treaded, there's no good way to choose one with proper rationale.

Either there are strong reasons to choose any one of them, or in my case, no particularly strong reason to choose Indian or Chinese food, or vice-versa.

I was stuck. I didn't know it at that time, But instead of rationale, if we take help from randomness to make a decision here, things can become much simpler.

We can flip a coin and randomly nudge the donkey thereby causing it to get closer to one source, either water or food, and accordingly away from the other. This way the impasse would be instantly broken, and the donkey will be either well fed then well hydrated, or well hydrated, then well fed.

Randomness to make a decision may seem like the opposite of reason or rationale—a form of giving up on a problem, the last resort.

But random outcomes can sometimes be used as a tool to break stalemates.

A man (or a donkey) who sees two options as truly equally compelling cannot be expected to be fully rational.

Sometimes the best solution to a problem is to turn to chance, rather than trying to fully reason out an answer.

In cricket, flipping a coin to help with the decision process of who should bat first is an example of using randomness usefully. This is efficient as long as a coin toss doesn't influence who would win or lose a match.

In our business, we see it happen regularly with investors.

FDs don't provide the inflation-beating returns and equities are perceived as too risky.

"The markets are too expensive, I will invest when they correct and after the correction, "they will fall further" are the common excuses we hear." They cannot decide where to invest, they miss the rally and the money remains in the savings account thereby losing the opportunity.

By the way, because I couldn't decide on which cuisine, I had to go to bed hungry that night.

Next time my wife puts me in a situation like this, all Iam going to do, is to flip a coin.

Decide either way, don't miss the opportunity, don't be a Buridan's donkey and stay blessed forever.

TAKE A BREAK – DISCONNECT TO RECONNECT

When Nobel prize-winning West Indian poet Derek Walcott was asked by an interviewer what he liked to do when he wasn't writing poetry, he said he liked to paint."Oh, I didn't realise you were an artist as well," said the interviewer.

"I'm not an artist," said the poet. "I don't paint pictures. I paint things—the walls of my house, my fence, my roof. It relaxes me."

What Walcott was talking about was something that many people who live on the outermost limits of consciousness—be The poets, scientists, and sages—have long realised: reach for the sky by all means; just remember to come down to earth after you've done so.

It's like a high-altitude mountaineer who, daring all dangers and difficulties, ventures into the thin cold air of the tallest of peaks.

Having taken in the all-embracing view that he commands from the lofty height that he has reached, the prudent mountaineer descends to the flatness of the plains, where the air is thick and heavy and dense with the oxygen that our bodies and our brains need to perform routine daily functions.

We can't forever live in the rarefied air of mountain tops or the pinnacles of consciousness; we must come down to the flatlands of daily reality to draw our breath and take comfort from the familiar and the predictable.
It's like an athlete, or a student studying hard for an exam. If the athlete trains too hard, or the student studies without the relief of a break, he will suffer burnout: the body and the mind, pushed to the limits and beyond of endurance, will seize up.

That's why poets paint their walls. Or why monks—be they Buddhist or Benedictine—who live the meditative life in monasteries ensure that they have a daily regimen of manual work: growing fruits and vegetables, keeping butter lamps lit, polishing stone and bronze.

Some achievers tend to their garden, some just take a walk, Some do menial home tasks and some find solace in cooking. So by all means excel in your chosen profession and work, meditate, lose yourself in the rapture of heightened consciousness.

Go after your dreams, work hard, and follow your passion, But don't forget that garden you still must tend to.Take a break, enjoy yourselves, that is equally important, And the weekend is the best time to disconnect to reconnect.

THE FOX AND THE CAT

In a certain forest there once lived a fox, and near to the fox lived a man who had a cat that had been a good mouser in its youth, but was now old and half blind. The man didn't want puss any longer, but not liking to kill it, took it out into the forest and lost it there. Then the fox came up and said, "Why, Mr Shaggy Matthew! How d'ye do! What brings you here?"––"Alas!" said Pussy, "my master loved me as long as I could bite, but now that I can bite no longer and have left off catching mice––and I used to catch them finely once––he doesn't like to kill me, but he has left me in the wood where I must perish miserably."––"No, dear Pussy!" said the fox; "you leave it to me, and I'll help you to get your daily bread."––"You are very good, dear little sister foxey!" said the cat, and the fox built him a little shed with a garden round it to walk about in.

Now one day the hare came to steal the man's cabbage. "Kreem- kreem-kreem!" he squeaked. But the cat popped his head out of the window, and when he saw the hare, he put up his back and stuck up his tail and said, "Ft-t-t-t-Frrrrrrr!" The hare was frightened and ran away and told the bear, the wolf, and the wild boar all about it. "Never mind," said the bear, "I tell you what, we'll all four give a banquet, and invite the fox and the cat, and do for the pair of them. Now, look here! I'll steal the man's mead; and you, Mr Wolf, steal his fat-pot; and you, Mr Wildboar, root up his fruit trees; and you, Mr Bunny, go and invite the fox and the cat to dinner."

So they made everything ready as the bear had said, and the hare ran off to invite the guests. He came beneath the window and said, "We invite your little ladyship Foxey-Woxey, together with Mr Shaggy Matthew, to dinner"––and back he ran again.––"But you should have told them to bring their spoons with them," said the bear.––"Oh, what a head I've got! if I didn't quite forget!" cried the hare, and back he went again, ran beneath the window and cried, "Mind you bring your spoons!"––"Very well," said the fox.

So the cat and the fox went to the banquet, and when the cat saw the bacon, he put up his back and stuck out his tail, and cried, "Mee-oo, mee-oo!" with all his might. But they thought he said, "Ma-lo, ma-lo!"––"What!" said the bear, who was hiding behind the beeches with the other beasts, "here have we four been getting together all we could, and this pig-faced cat calls it too little! What a monstrous cat he must be to have such an appetite!" So they were all four very frightened, and the bear ran up a tree, and the others hid where they could. But when the cat saw the boar's bristles sticking out from behind the bushes he thought it was a mouse, and put up his back again and cried, "Ft! ft! ft! Frrrrrrr!" Then they were more frightened than ever. And the boar went into a bush still farther off, and the wolf went behind an oak, and the bear got down from the tree and climbed up into a bigger one, and the hare ran right away.

But the cat remained in the midst of all the good things and ate away at the bacon, and the little fox gobbled up the honey, and they ate and ate till they couldn't eat any more, and then they both went home licking their paws.

HOPE!!

"We are born in one day. We die in one day. We can change
in one day. And we can fall in love in one day. Anything can
happen in just one day.
--GAYLE FORMAN"

This quote is the very basis for HOPE! When we remember what this quote says; the fact that anything really can happen in just one day, it gives us a reason to HOPE. It allows us to dream of something better and it motivates us to keep trying, it reminds us that wishes might still get granted and dreams might still come true.

So many people are struggling because they haven't found a job they badly need, because they haven't yet found the love of their life, or they haven't been able to have a child they desperately want or numerous other situations where they desire something that just hasn't happened yet, but the great thing is that all it takes is just one day for everything to change for the better, all it takes is just one day for everything you hope for to come true. Something good might happen one day but the happiness of that one day can change and your life would never be the same.

Again in one day or even a moment, something not so pleasant could also happen and give a lesson for a lifetime. Make the most of every day giving God thanks and glory for the chance to live, love, and grow to know what it is to be alive.

Don't give up hope. Don't stop working toward your dreams. Don't lose faith. Believe that anything is possible. Believe that anything can happen in just one day. And lucky for all of us, each night when we go to bed we get to wake up to another ONE DAY! And if tomorrow doesn't bring what you hope for, just remember, when you go to bed and then wake up again there will be yet another ONE DAY waiting for you and ONE DAY is all you need. Hang in there. Anything can happen in just one day.

THE LAW OF WASTED EFFORT

Do you know that Lions only succeed in a quarter of their hunting attempts - which means they fail in 75% of their attempts and succeed in only 25% of them? Despite this small percentage shared by most predators, they don't despair in their pursuit and hunting attempts. The main reason for this is not because of hunger as some might think but it is the understanding of the "Law of Wasted Efforts" that has been instinctively built into animals, a law by which nature is governed.

Half of the eggs of fishes are eaten... half of the baby bears die before puberty.- most of the world's rains fall in oceans-. and most of the seeds of trees are eaten by birds. Scientists have found that animals, trees, and other forces of nature are more receptive to the law of "wasted efforts".

Only humans think that the lack of success in a few attempts is a failure... but the truth is that: we only fail when we "stop trying". Success is not to have a life free of pitfalls and falls....but success is to walk over your mistakes and go beyond every stage where your efforts were wasted Look forward to the next
stage.

If there is a word that summarizes this world. it will simply be: Continue all over again!!!!
You can halt or take a rest momentarily but you cannot say QUIT, because success does not come after a few attempts of failure; you need to keep trying, never give up till you succeed, so learn to grow in your life at each stage and go beyond by understanding the Power of your Wasted Efforts.

CHAPTER ONE HUNDRED AND TEN

LIFE IS GOOD!

I would like to share a small but positive narrative. Bert and John Jacobs, the brothers who co-founded the $100 million Life Is Good T-shirt company, grew up as the youngest of six children in a lower-middle-class family in Boston.

When the brothers were in elementary school, their parents were in a near-death car accident from which their mother managed to escape with just a few broken bones — but their father lost the use of his right hand.

The stress and frustration from his physical therapy caused him to develop a harsh temper, they explain in their new book "Life Is Good."

"He did a lot of yelling when we were in grade school," John told Business Insider. And life certainly wasn't perfect. "There were often difficult things happening around the house," the brothers write.

But their mom, Joan, still believed life was good. So, every night as the family sat around the dinner table, she would ask her six kids to tell her something good that happened that day. "As simple as mom's words were, they changed the energy in the room," the brothers write. "Before we knew it, we were all riffing on the best, funniest, or most bizarre part of our day." John says that this daily exercise prevented them from developing a victim's mentality of "Oh, you wouldn't believe this horrible thing that happened to me today." Instead of griping about a teacher or homework assignment, he says that they would be laughing about a silly haircut a classmate got that day or a neat project they worked on at school.

"That optimism was something that our family always had, even when we had little else," they write.
Growing up with a mother like theirs — one who sang in the kitchen told animated stories and acted out children's books for them, no matter what bad situation they were going through — taught them an important lesson: Being happy isn't dependent on your circumstances.

"She showed us that optimism is a courageous choice you can make every day, especially in the face of adversity."They say her unwavering positive outlook on life is what inspired Life Is Good — their $100 million company the mission of which is to spread the power of optimism, with the tagline, "Life is not perfect. Life is not easy. Life is good." Since their mother's daily questions served them so well in life,
John says he and his brother now ask their employees the same thing when they all come together — "Tell me something good" — and the results have been positive. "It leads to ideas, which lead to progress, which leads to building on successes, instead of dwelling on challenges."
Life is Good!
Affirmation of the day :
My day begins and ends with gratitude.
Be grateful for this wonderful gift of Life!

NEVER STOP LEARNING

Today's story is about a painter who gave a very beautiful lesson to his son, the lesson which we can and we should learn from him. so come let's begin.

Once there was a painter, he was brilliant and was a veteran at his work he used to make his earning by selling his paintings and murals in the market, His earning by selling his depiction was about 15000$ monthly. So, he used to earn 500$ daily by selling one painting per day.

He was not poor but he was now growing old so he wanted to teach everything which he know about painting to his son. One night he called his son and explained to him everything about his condition that he is now growing old and he doesn't have that much power and strength to continue painting so he

told him that now you have to continue his business. His son was also ardent about painting so he complied with his father and decided to learn painting skills from his father.

Old painter trained his son, and taught him many things which are required to make paintings splendid. After two-three months of continued practice, his son was also able to make painting. After completing his masterpiece he decided to sell it on the market so the next day he went to the market and sold his painting for 100$. When he came back home his father became very happy that he sold his very first painting for 100 bucks but the son was not happy when his father asked him what is your reason to the sadness he told him that you use to sell your painting for 500$ and I sold mine for 100$. His father consolidated him and promised him that he will teach him more tricks, so after one month of training, he again painted one masterpiece and went to market, again he came back home with a sad face because this time he sold it for 200$ his father again trained him that which paint should be used and where which colour should be used, after a month of training he again sold and this time the son was very happy when he came back home, because this time he sold his painting for 700$ which was even more than the price of fathers painting which he used to sell, his father became elated from his son's success and told him that, so now you have reached this far, I will show you how to sell your painting for 1000$.

His son replied now I don't want to learn more because I have sold my painting more costly than you so you can't teach me anymore, after listening to the arrogant words from his son the old painter replied sorry to say son but your painting can't increase more in price from today, His son surprisingly asked him why then father replied to him that because, when I was young I also learned the painting skills from my father and one day I told him the same thing when I first sold my painting for 500$ because he use to sell his paintings for 300$. That was the biggest mistake of my life which ceased my progress because from that day I stopped learning.

His son realized his mistake apologized to his father and promised his father that he will never stop learning and he became a famous painter after that.

Moral: *It doesn't matter that the person who is lower in position than you or less educated than you or even smaller in age than you, don't think that he knows less than you, always learn from everyone regardless of his position or age.*

About The Author

Bramara Shivanna

Bramara Shivanna is an entrepreneur and enjoys helping women to become a better version of themselves to achieve success in their professional and social life.

Bramara Shivanna

Bramara Shivanna is an entrepreneur and enjoys helping women to become a better version of themselves to achieve success in their professional and social life.

She is an expert in Image management, Professional Grooming, Etiquette and Personal development training. She quit her job as a Software Engineer for a few years to raise her children and at the same time, she upgraded her skills and found her passion for helping women to become confident.

Bramara has a bachelor's degree in Telecommunication Engineering and also she has Post graduate diploma in Business Administration with a specialization in Human Resource Management, she worked as a Software developer for a decade.

Bramara is a Certified Image Consultant from Image Consulting Business Institute (ICBI), affiliated with the Conselle Institute of Image Management, USA. Train the Trainer (TTT) certification from the National Accreditation Board For Education and Training (NABET), One of the constituent boards of the Quality Council of India. A Certified Soft Skills Trainer from the Scottish Qualifications Authority (SQA).

Bramara runs a training and coaching institute Rhythmic image (www.rhythmicimage.com) as a solopreneur. She has helped hundreds of individuals with Grooming, etiquette, Image makeovers, Soft Skills and Personality development classes.

She conducts both Online and offline training for women and children both one-to-one coaching and group coaching. She conducts the "Smart Woman" program for women to enhance their external and inner personalities to achieve success in professional and social lives. She conducts a summer program for children by the name "Craft Your life" to achieve their goals.

Connect with us:
Email: - bramara@rhythmicimage.com
LinkedIn: - www.linkedin.com/in/bramarashivanna
Instagram: - @bramara_Rhythmicimage

About The Co Author

Meenakshi Ahuja

Meenakshi Ahuja

Meenakshi Ahuja, a leading Hospitality trainer in India has over 25 years of training experience and has trained more than 100 organisations in various fields of hospitality services. Apart from hospitality, she has conducted a wide range of workshops for the Indian Army, various Software and Manufacturing companies PAN-India and various Educational institutions. Ms Ahuja is one of the very few trainers in India, qualified to train individuals on Global Etiquette and Manners. Apart from being in senior management positions at various Hotels, she has also largely contributed to the food industry through her writings on food, recipes, hygiene and also being a Brand Ambassador for the RR Oomerbhoy Edible oils and Imported food products. Her writings have also covered areas of grooming, hygiene, and recipes, in periodicals like the TOI and The Indian Express and Mid-Day. A strong believer in Quality Management Education /through a flexible and industry-oriented curriculum that caters both to full-time students & working populace and increases the employability of the students.

Her OUTSTANDING ACHIEVEMENTS Miss Bangalore & First Runner-up Miss India - 1971 Finalist: WILLS Made for Each Other Contest- 1971 Won Prizes for Cookery Shows, Flower Arrangements and other Interior's related decorations & arrangements.

She has co-authored " SANDWICHES (Toasted, Plain Grilled)" and authored "Non-Vegetarian Chinese Cooking" books.

FOR WORKSHOPS AND LECTURES ON SUBJECTS mentioned below mail to: mamahuja@gmail.com:-

Behavioural Skills, Overall development, Image Management, Communication Skills, Body Language, Train-the-Trainer workshops, Anger management, Communication skills, Soft Skills, Pageant Training on Soft Skills, Persuasive Communication, Interviewing Skills, Personality Development, Confidence Building and many more.

She has conducted workshops for these Organizations: IATA, City Pride School, CYDA, Team Konnect Consultancy, SP Jain International College of Military Engineering, National Defense Academy (NDA), Institute of Armament Technology, Armed Forces Medical College (AFMC) and Bombay Engineering Group (BEG) - at Pune IAS Training Academy, Mussoorie Dina Institute DY Patil College Indira Institute of Management Abida Inamdar College Singhad Technical Education Society ...and others Workshops &Lectures conducted at Educational Institutes & colleges:

Connect with us:-

Email:- mamahuja@gmail.com

Linkedin:- https://www.linkedin.com/in/meenakshi-ahuja-0276539

Facebook:- https://www.facebook.com/meenakshi.ahuja

Instagram:- https://instagram.com/ahujameenakshi?igshid=YmMyMTA2M2Y=

The Art of Personal Grooming

Bramara is an experienced image consultant and spent years studying Image Management, Etiquette, Grooming and Visual communication. In the book "The art of personal grooming" she gives expert advice on every aspect of personal grooming for women to look well-groomed and polished. This is the first book in the Smart Woman Series.

The Art of Personal Grooming

The book is based on the three pillars of personal grooming. It covers every aspect of personal hygiene and grooming habits in a simple way and also explains the causes of bad grooming and its prevention. The importance of grooming in creating a good impression is explained with suitable examples. Few chapters are dedicated exclusively to the basics of dressing, makeup, and accessories. You can learn secrets of levels of dressing for both Indian and western corporate attire along with the perceived message for each level of dressing. The book covers corporate dressing and makeup tips and their benefits. All the myths associated with grooming and a step-by-step workable plan for grooming routine are included.

This book effectively shows you how to put your best foot forward and look Well-Groomed and polished for every occasion by coordinating your outfits with matching accessories along with a suitable hairstyle and good grooming. This book is for every woman who aspires to look competent and confident and would like to elevate their look, specifically for women professionals, women attending job interviews, a trainer, entrepreneurs, a mother who wishes to look well-groomed and standout.

Sources And Citiations

Dear Reader

I have tried to keep this book error free. But if errors have crept in do let me know. The images and content used in this book are sourced from various internet sources shared by many unknown people circulated in various whats app groups and a few stories were written by Meenakshi Ahuja madam. None of the stories is written by me. I collected the stories and compiled them as a book so that everyone can access this knowledge for their self-development.

Thank you for buying this book.

All trademarks and brands referred to in this book are for illustrative purposes only, are the property of their respective owners and are not affiliated with this publication in any way. Any trademarks are being used without permission, and the publication of the trademark is not authorized by, associated with or sponsored by the trademark owner.

Epilogue

" "In the long run, we shape our lives, and we shape ourselves. The process never ends until we die. And the choices we make are ultimately our own responsibility."

—Eleanor Roosevelt "